It is not an overstatement to say th⸺ ⸺ ⸺ anged my life. During my time there b ⸺ ⸺ lirector, I grew in so many ways—ways ⸺ to grow in. I made friends who would ⸺ ⸺ ⸺ ⸺ uilt on the firm foundation of Jesus, whon ⸺ ⸺ can call for advice, support, or celebration. At the student center, the faith of a prideful young boy was nurtured, challenged, and sharpened into the faith of a (more) mature young man. I have often said that the student center was the closest thing to the community we read about in Acts 2 that I have ever experienced. Though I will always have room to grow, I can truly credit this crucial time in my life for shaping the trajectory toward a mature faith that I continue to attempt to follow today, led by the Spirit.

Now ten years have passed since we began, but Craig remains at the helm, fighting the spiritual battle for each class of college students that comes through the doors of the student center, and I love him for it. This book is the culmination of Craig's past decade of experience working with college students. He has had ten years of conversations with these young adults that fall across the full spectrum of faith, from nominal to completely committed, as well as outside of this spectrum. He has tried and tested methods of interacting with and teaching students and found some to be more effective than others.

In this book, he traces through highs and lows of his time at the student center to condense what he has learned into practical words of wisdom for anyone who is concerned about the faith of young adults. I can attest to the true power that these methods hold to build and sustain faith. Craig uses his experience to give us insight into the lives and minds of college students amid a battle of faith. Many of the methods apply not just to college students—we all would do well to apply them in our lives no matter what stage of life we are in. Not all the methods will work in every situation, but the general framework that Craig lays out in this book can be adapted as necessary to apply the practical wisdom that he has gained in the past decade at the student center to. strengthen our spiritual walk. I pray that these words will be a blessing to you, and that the application of these words will help you grow to be more like Jesus every day.

Walter Harrington, PhD, postdoctoral research associate, Department of Infectious Diseases, St. Jude Children's Research Hospital

The Lion, the Way, and the War is a practical take on ministry in the twenty-first century. Allison uses his extensive history of analyzing data in the secular world juxtaposed with his experiences in ministry to correlate a practical game plan that can be useful to parents, ministers, and teachers alike. In this ministry field guide, Allison isn't afraid to tackle difficult topics pertaining to the sustainability of a young person's faith post high school graduation. He includes the role of parents in shaping a child's relationship to the church and the Savior. In addition to fact-based discussions, Allison uses his personal experiences as a campus minister at a large state university to suggest successful practices that can be carried out in any ministry. His thought-provoking ideas help form a mindset for waging battle against the worldly enemies of young people today. This book is a noteworthy addition to the library of anyone concerned about teens and young adults as well as about the future of the Lord's church.

Cody Harrington, MA, Ministerial Counseling, youth minister, Ethridge, Tennessee

The Lion, the Way, and the War is a huge call to action. Craig's statements are bold, and his determination for a spiritual movement is not for the faint of heart. This book should encourage and push every church to look at themselves and reevaluate. Whom are we trying to please? What is the goal? If the answer is not Jesus, it may be time for a change. Change is scary, but the reward of salvation is much greater than any fear. This book in particular points out the fight for the faith in our youth, which is extremely important. Our youth is the only way to continue the work Jesus started in His ministry here on earth. They are the next generation of Christians who will teach the next generation, and so on. Our goal should be set on getting them involved and pouring into these individuals. If we lose sight of this goal, we may not be fulfilling what God has called us to do. I have been involved in the Christian Student Center as a student for two years and a Student Ambassador for two years. In these four years, I have learned more than I could have ever imagined about Christ, myself, and the church. I have never found a place like the CSC. A place that is completely dedicated day in and day out to the work of God. Craig talks about the importance of our setup, why we are successful in bringing each other up, and ways to mimic this in your own church setting. Our mission, dedication, and work are the things I hope to take with me everywhere I go. My life has forever been touched and changed by the Christian Student Center.

Blair Shelton, former student ambassador, UTC, Christian Student Center

The Lion, the Way, and the War addresses a major problem facing our church today: lost souls during the transition to college. It gives tangible ways to evaluate where we are going wrong and how to combat the enemy. All of this is structured around how a Christian student center that I attended operates. The CSC, as we lovingly call it, was my life during my time at the University of TN at Chattanooga. The faith, love, and trust shown within those walls caused me to reevaluate my life to a true spiritual reawakening. I had gone to church my entire life, but my faith was not my own until I was discipled there. I was empowered to dig deeper and discover the true meaning in every scripture all while growing with fellow brothers and sisters in Christ.

This book describes the importance of this time for young Christians as well as the importance of the foundation during childhood. If you would like to be part of the solution, this book will be invaluable. Reading it has caused me to reexamine what I have done since leaving the CSC, and I definitely plan to follow some of the structures outlined. We truly must band together as one church to edify and disciple our youth because the implications are everlasting.

Ashlee King, DVM

When Paul describes what the relationship between teachers, shepherds, and even the apostles and the church body should look like in Ephesians 4:11–14, he more than implied that there should be a maturity and fullness that we should all reach from this relationship with leadership in the church. Those who serve in the roles responsible for this equipping are called to be good stewards over the spiritual "successes" and "failures" they see directly from their instruction so the body of Christ grows into a mature unity of faith that can withstand the schemes of Satan. We see this in action in the writing of *The Lion, the Way, and the War*. Parents, and even leaders, would be considered wise to embrace the precepts Craig Allison lays out here. With over ten years of experience as a college campus minister, Craig has written out proven experience in strengthening the faith of our youth beyond a shallow, spiritless youth experience found in most churches today.

Chris Turner, elder

The Christian Student Center under Craig's leadership shifted my paradigm of what it means to be a participant in the Christian faith. From someone who did not experience church until my late teens, I was a babe in Christ when I first stepped through the doors of the Christian Student Center. I was challenged to grow and mature my spiritual and personal life. I made friendships that became family and built my first relationships that were centered around our Savior. The Christian Student Center was the closest thing I have ever encountered to the Christian faith that we read about in Acts 2.

As someone who served in the role of a youth minister at a congregation immediately after my time at the Christian Student Center, I can assure you that there is a serious spiritual battle that high school and college students face every day. Craig uses his years of experience, insight, and wisdom gained from interacting with our youth as the campus minister to call Christ's church to action. The methods and ideology found in *The Lion, the Way, and the War* create a scripturally grounded and effective framework that answers one of our biggest issues in the church: "Why is our youth walking away from their Christian faith?" If you are a parent, minister, elder, deacon, or anyone who is concerned about the biggest obstacle facing our church today, I encourage you to read this book. In essence, this book provides practical and effective techniques to construct and support a Christ-centered faith, while also providing useful strategies that counter the departure of our youth from their faith walk.

Brandon Bonner, former student ambassador and youth minister

CRAIG P. ALLISON

THE
LION
THE
WAY
AND THE
WAR

The Battle for Our Youth's Spiritual
Salvation in a Postmodern World

Cover and interior design: YouPublish (youpublish.com)

To my wife, Betsye, and my children,
Harrison, Kailey, and Parker.

CONTENTS

ACKNOWLEDGEMENTS

This book would not be possible without the encouragement, help, and input of numerous individuals.

My wife is a constant source of knowledge and inspiration. My best thoughts and ideas begin and end with you. The many sacrifices you have made, your support of me, and the Christian Student Center (CSC), the complete chaos that is our home with college students constantly in and out . . . nothing or no one could have prepared us for this journey, and I thank God that you have been the one beside me through it all.

Likewise, my three kids, Harrison, Kailey, and Parker have grown up in the CSC and have had to share their dad with hundreds of other kids. They have served as my sounding board for the ideas that pop into my brain, and to their credit always told me when my ideas needed to be tossed.

To my parents, Pat and Barbara, who are the best examples of living out one's faith as I have ever seen. They represent the entire backdrop of this book and how I want to approach my relationship with Christ.

To Chris Turner and Brent Clark who have held me accountable and challenged me to dig deeper into God's Word every Monday at 1:30.

To David Schonhoff and my church family at Central in Chattanooga who have stood by me these last ten years and supported the work at the CSC.

To all the students at the CSC and especially to all the student directors/student ambassadors who have helped mold and shape the ministry at UTC and have been part of my personal small groups. This book would not be here without you so I want to acknowledge each of you: Walter Harrington, Miranda Trentle, Tiffany Reed, Lily Sanchez, Rachel Neill, Shelton Neill, Trevor Reish, Aubrey Davis, Luke Davis, Clark Boshers, Erin Boshers, Katherine Buchanan, Ben Buchanan, Nick Priquette, Jordan Grindell, Stephanie Crouse, Kelsey Thrash, Kaitlyn Coots, Sara VanSenus, Alex VanSenus, Will Day, Ashlee King, Katherine Mimms, Greg Howell, Harrison Foster, Kaleb McDowd, Brenna Barry, Brenna Yap, Cody Harrington, Chynna Harrington, Cody Hedgecoth, Ashley Holloway, Chris Matherly, Macy Partin, Brandon Bonner, Harrison Allison, Lexie Bonner, Jeremy Handzel, Katie Stofel, Kara Stofel, Sophie Barton, Megan Scalf, Kristen McCampbell, Laura King, Blair Shelton, Bobby Holden, Evan Johnson, Hunter Hayes, Morgan Bowser, Kate Large, Chris Barrow, Chance Hobbs, Josh Boshers, Preston Johnson, Raylee Colwell, Kynzie Walker, Emma Stidham, and Tynan Breeds. Without your help, we would not be the ministry that we are. I pray for you often.

To Wanda and Gary Mance, you have been beside me since day one, and I cherish your support and wise counsel over the years. The work the two of you have put in at the CSC, all the retreats, the thousands upon thousands of meals that you have prepared, and the hundreds of students who have benefited from your advice and wisdom cannot be overstated. Wanda, your imprint on the CSC is one of the greatest blessings to this mission work. If there is a legacy to be remembered here, it is the one that you have created.

Finally, the real reason this book was written is because of Jesus. He is the only one who matters in the great scheme of things. We owe Him everything because He is our everything. Nothing exists that did not come through Him first. Without Jesus, we are less than nothing, but because HE IS, we are given the opportunity to enjoy momentary glimpses of the spectacular while awaiting a home where we will enjoy eternal glory.

INTRODUCTION

Why This Book?

Thank you for picking up this copy of *The Lion, the Way, and the War.* Now that it is in your hands, you may be wondering, *Is this something I need to read?* Let me answer that question right now and perhaps save you some time and money. This is a book intended to be read by parents, youth ministers, college ministers, and church leaders who have been searching for proven methods and strategies to help their high school and college students hang on to their faith. This is a book that will provide insight into why church growth is stagnating, why our youth are leaving the church after they leave home, and the battle that is on our doorstep. More importantly, within these pages a tangible strategy is provided to counter Satan's attack on our youth and the church. In fact, one will read about a program that has resulted in the majority of college students connecting to their faith and to God in ways that are notable in scope, number, and sustainability. By sustainability I mean those students who have graduated college and are actively pursuing God and working to share the gospel with others. Understand that the future of the church is dependent on our youth maintaining their faith. Satan knows this, and that is the reason he is waging war on that specific demographic. Our youth are being attacked in ways that most parents and churches may not realize. Perhaps you are only seeing the aftermath of the attack and have grave concerns. Perhaps you have seen with your own eyes that the church is in peril as you watch two out of every three young people leave and not come back, and you have no idea how to stop our kids from walking away.

This book is the culmination of over ten years of trial and error, interviews, observations, research, and study to develop a methodology that addresses the gaps that have cultivated an atmosphere of apathy in our homes, youth programs, college ministries, and churches. As a campus minister working at a large state university in Tennessee, I see the direct results that parents and churches have had on their youth. I get to witness the effectiveness (or ineffectiveness) of many different parenting styles and church programs aimed at keeping kids connected to their faith once they leave home. Sadly, from my research, perspective and observations, we are failing. I want you to see what I see, to know what I know, and understand what needs to start happening so that you can help me in this fight for our youth. As you read, it may surprise you to learn that the methodology used to win souls back to Christ is not new. The purpose is to bring back first-century discipling methods demonstrated by Jesus instead of using the vast array of current cultural gimmicks being used by hundreds of churches and ministries. As a result of going back to a biblical example, I have witnessed a major decrease in the hemorrhaging of our youth's souls to the world. While the methods are not new, the way I have implemented my approach may be considered radical by some when looking through a twenty-first-century lens. Even so, I am excited to share this "radical" approach with you.

You may be wondering, *What is the success rate and how have you measured and tracked those numbers?* While there is some subjectivity to that answer, there are many leading indicators that provided data points to consider along this journey. Though the objective elements are good to examine, it is important not to get pulled into a "numbers only" mentality. The more important consequences of faith growth will remain our focus and will be thoroughly addressed throughout these pages. That answers for whom this book was written and touches on what this book is about. The last area to address in these opening remarks is why I wrote this book.

Let me first start by saying that I do not presume to have all the answers, nor do I think the methods presented here are the only ones that could be used to wage war against Satan, although they have proven to be extremely effective. Further, I am not suggesting that if your son or daughter fails to connect with a Christian ministry while in college they are destined to walk away from their faith. The primary objective in writing this book is to share a program that is defeating our enemy in big ways. I understand that is a bold claim, but I am excited to share the valuable lessons that have been learned and what I continue to witness as more young people are empowered to break the chains of the world and earnestly connect with Christ in ways that exemplify first-century Christianity. By sharing these insights, my prayer is you will find similar success in your home, church, and ministries.

There are three time periods in a child's life that will have a major impact on their faith as an adult. The time the child is at home (especially the high school years), during college, and immediately after college. If high school youth ministry has a program that lacks in substance, then transitioning to college ministry becomes unlikely. The same is true of college ministry. Those that lack substance produce weak Christians who will most likely drift away after college. As such, if young adults fail to connect and grow their faith while in college, one cannot expect them to engage in a church after college. If the next generation is not connecting with their faith and spirituality, the church should not be surprised to see a continued decrease in their numbers.

Sadly, that is exactly what the research indicates. Church attendance is in decline. According to a 2021 Gallup article, author Jeffrey Jones reports that, "Americans' membership in houses of worship continued to decline last year, dropping below 50% for the first time in Gallup's eight-decade trend."[1] Consider the steady rate of decline in the graphic below:

Church Membership Among U.S. Adults Now Below 50%

Do you happen to be a member of a church, synagogue or mosque?

— % Yes, member

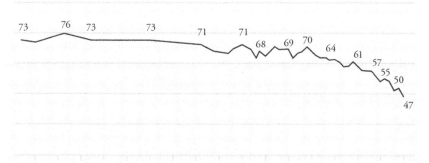

Based on annual aggregated data, usually based on two surveys
GALLUP

Most of us in the church are failing to recognize that these three critical phases of a young person's life should not be viewed independently. They are connected, and one feeds the next. So it is within this holistic paradigm that a methodology providing the basis to create the proper environments for growth within all three time periods was needed. If such a book exists, I have failed to find it. Hopefully, this void will now be filled by the text you are holding.

During the COVID shutdown in 2020, a leader from within the church and a good friend of mine said that I needed to put down in writing what was happening within our program so others could benefit from it. That, in essence, is why I have written this book. The gospel has not lost its power, and our leadership team at the CSC has found that the discipling techniques used in the first-century church is still the most effective way to bring others to Christ as well as enabling an atmosphere of growth in one's faith. We believe that one of the primary issues is that the church in general and parents specifically have strayed from the simplicity we read about in Acts 2. So many churches have felt the need to create atmospheres that they believe will attract our youth. While their efforts are to be commended, their approach has fallen short. In fact, these efforts are hurting more than they are helping. At the end of the day, we need to be about the work of building Christ followers who will disciple others, who, in turn, will disciple others. Over the last decade I have seen several common themes emerge that are responsible for the hemorrhaging of our churches. This book will discuss the cause of these wounds in detail and provide tangible ways to stop the bleeding.

I want to thank you for picking up a copy of *The Lion, the Way, and the War*. That means you recognize the church is facing a dilemma . . . one that cannot be ignored any longer. The stakes are too high, and we need answers that actually work—not theories, gimmicks, or unproven methods. The answer is simple and is the same answer it has always been: the *Lion* of Judah, our Savior, Jesus the Christ. Make no mistake: our youth and the church (called the *Way* in the New Testament) are under a new and fierce attack by Satan, and he is experiencing tremendous success. The *War* has already begun. It is time to start fighting back in earnest.

PART 1

THE WHEEL

Before I began the work of campus ministry, I spent about twenty years working for large corporations in a variety of roles. The majority of this time I worked as an environmental, health, and safety professional. I quickly learned that in the business world, the main priority is profit. Profit is the god of business and companies thrive or die based on profit. As such, millions of dollars are invested by companies to figure out how to be profitable, and this almost always involves the deployment of business models and strategies. The most effective models are those that can take the complexity of the many moving parts required to run a large organization and create a model through which one can envision how all the moving parts fit together to make the whole. In short, simplifying that which is complex. What we mean by this is how the complexity and vastness of God's redemptive plan may be difficult for us to comprehend, but when viewed through the model He gave us (Jesus Christ), that which is complex is understood. *We see a clear model of love, obedience, humility, and submission exemplified through Jesus.*

So when we begin to examine the critical issue of the church losing its youth to the world, we discover many variables ranging in complexity. One of my goals is to help parents and churches grasp the big picture and understand how the many variables are connected in a way that is manageable, teachable, and sustainable. This includes the issues as well as the solutions. With that objective in mind, I will be using a very simple model: the wheel. Imagine an old-fashioned wagon wheel with three primary components. The outer wheel, the spokes, and the center hub. Something like this:

The goal of the wheel is to carry a load and to do so while moving from one location to another in the most efficient manner possible. Our study begins by looking first at the outer wheel. Without the outer wheel, movement would be impossible. The spokes would be free to drift and wobble. They would be unstable and without consistency. If you tried to move the wheel without the outer circle, the end of the spokes would simply become stuck in the ground. All movement would abruptly stop, and other spokes could snap or break in half. Our model will suggest that parents are the primary builders of the outer wheel for their children, and the church is a secondary reinforcement of the outer wheel. These two components (home and church) work together in a symbiotic relationship. They provide the necessary foundation and reinforcement that keeps all the spokes in line and secure. However, based upon our observations and interviews over the last decade with parents and teens, this system is no longer working in conjunction. As with any good strategy, it is important to understand the problem and the issues that contribute to the failure. But first, let's discuss the rest of the wheel.

The spokes, which are connected to both the outer wheel and the hub, represent the various components of our Christian journey. Finally, at the center of the wheel is the hub, which is the source of strength and the foundation of the entire wheel. This center is of course, Jesus Christ.

There are areas that have emerged as targets where Satan is directing his attention to break the symbiotic relationship between the parents, their children, and the church. If Satan gains a foothold in any one of these areas, the results are widespread and cause major damage to a young person's spiritual foundation. Briefly, these points of attack include youth ministry, church leadership, isolationism, technology, and moral relativism. I want to ask the reader to pause for just a moment and think critically about these five topics. In the decade I have researched this issue, almost every victory by Satan is because he has utilized youth ministry, church leadership, the drift into isolationism brought on by our modern world, technology, and the infiltration of moral relativism into our educational systems. Youth ministry and church leadership can be grouped together. They are both components of the church. By working to manipulate church leadership, Satan can remain unobserved as he pushes subtle agendas that eventually create issues of complacency. By attacking youth ministry, Satan uses a variety of methods to derail spiritual maturity in our youth. The interdependency between these two areas will be examined in more detail.

The other three areas are also connected in subtle ways that were so clever, many parents failed to see the danger until it was too late. Because of social media platforms, teens have become more isolated than at any other time in history. Further, our children are bombarded with the message that morality is subjective. They see this message repeated every day through social media, friends, teachers, the entertainment industry, and society. The concept of "truth" is whatever each individual person says it is. I have literally heard hundreds of college students tell me, "Your truth is your truth, and my truth is my truth, and both are correct." They believe this lie completely through what I call "conviction by repetition." The moment our kids gained access to the internet, our world opened a vast chasm, and we still do not know how far down this hole will take us. This is something that most parents, churches, and youth ministries are failing to address. So to begin, I would like to start by discussing the different components that make the outer wheel, which is comprised of the home and church. To do this we will examine the five components that Satan is targeting to destroy both home and church. We will start with youth ministry.

1

YOUTH MINISTRY: SHIFTING RESPONSIBILITY

The history of youth ministry and paid youth ministers within churches has not always existed. In fact, youth ministry is a relatively new invention and addition to churches. The creation of youth ministry has produced three major risk factors.

First, youth ministry has ushered in a new set of expectations from parents. The responsibility for teaching children about spiritual matters has shifted from the home to the youth minister, and it was as though a collective sigh of relief could be heard across Christendom as this massive responsibility fell onto another person's shoulders. Sure, there may have been some initial concerns as parents handed over the reins, but these concerns were pacified by the assurance from church leaders that having a youth minister would greatly enhance the parent's spiritual work being done in the home, and they may have been correct . . . initially. Like most new programs, the newness eventually fades, and complacency begins to creep in. Parents began to see that school schedules were demanding more time from their children and extracurricular activities were becoming more prevalent. There was a time, not too long ago, when ball practice would never have been scheduled for a Wednesday night simply because school administers knew that most people had a midweek service at church. There was a time when church attendance was seen as a value adding practice, so measures were taken

27

to protect those practices. It may seem stranger still that many businesses closed on Sundays.

We all know these days are gone. Not only do schools actively schedule practices on Wednesdays but they also have games on Sundays. Parents who want their children to have a robust experience in middle and high school, who want their kids to experience team sports, often must choose between ballgames and church. I have two personal experiences that underscore the pervasiveness of this new reality. Stay with me for a moment as I diverge because this example, as you will see, correlates with youth ministry.

My wife and I were naïve in thinking that enrolling our children in a private Christian school would protect them (and us) from the pressures of choosing between secular extracurricular activities and our church activities. Unfortunately, we discovered the world's value on church attendance had infiltrated a Christian-based education system. Of greater concern, we knew of several church leaders within our community whose family regularly skipped worship services to watch their kids compete in sports activities instead of attending Sunday worship. This was not an infrequent practice. Those Christians who tell their children that God is the number one priority in their lives yet regularly replace worship with ballgames should consider the question: What is the long-term impact this message has on our youth?

Before I became a campus minister, I would not have been able to answer that question. I heard the arguments in favor of ballgames. "It's only for a season. We only miss church once in a while. They are learning important life lessons, such as how to be a team player. They are developing social skills. They may use this activity to invite their friends to church." There are more, but you probably get the gist.

In all honesty, these arguments sounded plausible, and I was not able to see how these decisions impacted our children once they left home. But now I do, and I need to tell you (the parent) that you are making a horrible mistake by substituting games for God. Even doing it one time sends a message to your children. I know this because your kids tell me about the confusion they felt and how the excuses you made for missing church sounded hollow, weak, and disingenuous. In other words, they saw the lie for what it was, but you were the parent, and they followed your lead. The hypocrisy became an itch they could not scratch, and it drove many of them into a spiritual crisis. Do you not know that Satan was watching for just such an opening—a gap that he could exploit and exploit it he did!

I have often wondered why so many parents have so easily succumbed to the pressures of this world and put worldly things before godly things. As I contemplate this trend, the words of the apostle Paul in 2 Timothy 4:1–4 come to mind:

> I charge you in the presence of God and of Christ Jesus, who
> is to judge the living and the dead, and by his appearing and
> his kingdom, preach the word; be ready in season and out of
> season; reprove, rebuke, and exhort, with complete patience and
> teaching. For the time is coming when people will not endure
> sound teaching, but having itching ears they will accumulate for
> themselves teachers to suit their own passions, and will turn away
> from listening to the truth and wander off into myths.

Is it any wonder then, as we consider this one particular example, that if parents have grown complacent and surrendered the spiritual priorities of their children to the school systems, that they would not have done the same to their youth minister? As an added reason to justify this surrender, parents will further appease a guilty conscience by reminding themselves and others that the church is paying for a youth minister. In effect, "Teaching my kids the spiritual stuff is what we pay them to do."

I realize this wording sounds harsh, and it was my intention to make it sound that way for a reason. Here is why: The reality, as in most cases where plans go bad, is a system where slow, incremental changes have occurred over time, almost beyond our perception to notice them.

Then one day we wake up and realize that we, as parents, have handed over our most important job to someone else. It is not reasonable to expect that our children will have a faith that produces the kind of fruit Jesus expects to see when we have capitulated their spiritual education to a couple of hours each week to the youth minister. It is not a fair expectation for our youth ministers, and it is not a fair expectation for our children. When parents spend more time on Netflix (or any other screen) than they do in conversation and study with their children about God, the outcome is inevitable.

I hope you can recognize the foundation of youth ministry that we have created and nurtured over time. Youth ministry is not what it used to be. New youth ministers graduating from Christian universities do not appear to comprehend the gravity of the situation and how most of the curriculum they are being taught is not only irrelevant but also dangerous to sustaining the faith of our youth.

Before I go further, and lest one thinks we should go fire every youth minister tomorrow, I am not opposed to youth ministry. In our current society, parents need all the help they can get. We need every tool, every resource, and every opportunity to provide Christian examples, Christian environments, and Christian development that will counter what your children are being exposed to in the world. So yes, youth ministers play an important role in your child's spiritual journey, but they are supplemental, not primary.

And that is my point. The roles have become reversed, and this is the trend that has been observed over the last decade. But that is not what is being taught anymore. Youth ministers enter their jobs with the expectation that they are your children's main spiritual influencer. They think they are the ones who are supposed to provide most of our youth's spiritual education. This is wrong. More importantly, it is unbiblical. Ephesians 6:4 clearly intends for a child's parents to be the primary source of instruction regarding Jesus.

The solution is not difficult. Church leaders, parents, and youth ministers must come together and discuss who is supposed to do what.

The majority of teaching should be happening at home. The youth minister is introducing topical studies and providing resources and materials to the parents as the discussion points for nightly Bible studies. When the children come back into the church Bible study with the youth minister, they are bringing with them the profound insights gained from the in-home discussions. It is a sharpening of iron. It is a synergistic model that promotes higher levels of learning. In turn, the leadership of the church supports this system, encourages the parents to do their part, and even holds parents accountable for the spiritual growth of their kids. Talk about a paradigm shift! This system is not impossible to implement, but like anything worthwhile, it will require effort and a radical way of approaching how we view the primary function of youth ministers.

Second, youth ministry in many congregations has created segregation. Youth programs are inherently set up to segregate kids not only from the church at large but also within their own youth program. Granted, it does not always make sense to have middle school kids in with high school kids, especially with the more mature subject matter that emerges in late teens. However, there is a great benefit in providing regular opportunities for the youth to engage all age demographics. We often hear, "The future of the church is our youth," and while there is truth in this statement, the reality is the youth is part of the church now. When I come across college students who have a faith beyond their years, a spiritual wisdom and maturity that is meaningful and deep, I almost always find that this student has been included in their home church in multiple ways.

Consider these questions:

- Does your church invite your youth to regularly participate in worship?
- Does your preacher preach sermons geared only to an adult age demographic?

- Do your church leaders invite their youth to be a part of any church committees? Does your church value their youth to the point of being intentional with intergenerational connections?
- How big of a change would it be to invite your youth to be part of an outreach planning committee (or a VBS), to help organize a giveaway, or to help prepare meals for the homeless?

When we box in our youth to a certain tradition or paradigm, we segregate them from the church, and they will eventually feel disconnected with their church family. Most of them will leave after high school simply because they did not feel like they mattered or that they were an integral part of the church. We seem to think the important roles of church are reserved for the older members.

Third, youth ministry has become extremely susceptible to "spiritual fads." For example, a conversation I had with a new youth minister went something like this:

"Hi, Mark. It's Craig. I saw you guys have a few seniors that are graduating from high school this year and may be interested in coming to our university. Was wondering if you might share my contact information with them and get us connected? I'd really like for them to know about our campus ministry before they enroll."

"Oh . . . yeah, well . . . I'm not really sure how excited they would be to get involved in a campus ministry. To be honest, they aren't really plugged in with our youth program here."

"Really? What do you mean?"

"Well, they love to come to all the fun activities. Seems like they always show up for those events, but they are never here for the Bible studies or for class."

"I'm sorry to hear that. So, I'm curious, Mark. Would you say you all do more fun stuff or do you have more Bible studies and classes to really dig deep into God's Word?"

"Look, I'm not sure what you're asking. I mean, you know how kids are today. The only way to get them to show up for anything is to basically bribe them with food and games, and sometimes that's not even enough. Plus, I'm expected to have so many events each month, and the parents are always complaining about something . . ."

If you are a youth minister, this may sound familiar. For most congregations, youth ministry has devolved into a church-sponsored babysitting club that provides pizza, entertainment, and occasional field trips. Every church is competing to see who can get the best pizza, have the most relevant entertainment, and take the greatest field trips. Successful youth ministry is now measured by a head count rather than a heart count. Lots of kids implies the youth program must be working in the eyes of the church.

Unfortunately, this focus on entertainment has also bled into many worship settings that serve to reinforce the idea that faith growth is dependent on popular culture that seeks constant spiritual highs. When worship resembles a high school pep rally, church leaders have failed their membership, especially their youth. In Rod Dreher's book *The Benedict Option*, he states, "Contemporary worship manipulates. God is not a fad or a hipster deity. To attach him to our own little slice of popular culture fails to do justice to him as the transcendent God over all history and cultures."[2]

This attitude carries over to college ministry too. It is as though each opportunity to plant deep spiritual roots in our children's lives are quickly discarded to bring in larger crowds as evidence of success! I talked to a college minister, and he told me how many students he had at a worship event. Over a hundred. He bragged about the popular praise band he had managed to book and described the anticipation building up to a concert-style event. I asked him how many extemporaneous, student-led Bible studies were taking place each week. He looked at me like I had grown a second head.

There is a growing fundamental truth. While an emotionally driven worship that uses elements of a rock concert are effective in producing a temporary emotional high, emerging research indicates that this does not produce long-lasting spiritual roots.[3] In fact, it has the opposite effect. But this is the part that goes unnoticed. And if you happen to speak to the facts, you may be labeled as "legalistic" or, even worse, "judgmental."

What parents, youth ministers, and churches do not see is what happens after these kids, who have been fed spiritual junk food for twelve years, graduate from high school. There is nothing worse than seeing the malnourished soul of a young person who had every opportunity to enter college as an ambassador for Christ but instead comes through our doors expecting to be entertained. When they realize that we are a ministry without the loudness of the world, they usually seek out a ministry that employs the very same cacophony they are used to hearing. Make no mistake. This is the very noise that deafened them in high school, and it is the same noise that blocks their ears from hearing what God wants them to hear. Being deaf to His voice, they eventually give up and walk away from what little faith they had.

So what does a person like Mark, the youth minister, do in this situation? Our advice is this: Toss your program out the window and start over. Call an emergency meeting with the parents and church leaders and tell them what is at stake (the souls of the children) and why an immediate change is needed. Numbers do not matter. This is a matter of the heart, the mind, and the spirit. Some of the largest high school youth ministries—largest meaning the number of students attending—do not meet the definition of success. What are we really talking about here? I understand some will disagree with me on these points, but I'm convinced, based on thousands of conversations with college students, that if we take stock of what the primary function of youth ministers should be, and what high school kids really need to see and hear, we will arrive at the same conclusion.

Simply stated, a youth minister's primary job, more than anything else, is to introduce their students to Jesus. Perhaps you are thinking, *That sounds a bit obvious. Doesn't everyone in the US already know who Jesus is?* And you would be correct in thinking that. But it has been my experience that even though everyone knows who Jesus is, they do not know *who* Jesus is to them. They know who Jesus is to their church. They know who Jesus is to their parents or family. They know who Jesus is to friends. But they really don't know who Jesus is to them, and they don't think it really matters.

Coming to know Jesus for oneself is the biggest, single life-changing event of our lives. Coming to one's own faith in Christ is a whole different ballgame than practicing your parent's faith. Riding the coattails of a parent's faith is, in fact, the leftovers. Jesus doesn't expect us to eat leftovers. He wants us to have the main entrée. And that is what youth ministers need to be teaching, showing, and demonstrating to their students, and the parents need to be supporting this agenda wholeheartedly.

What does it really mean to have a successful youth ministry that is properly preparing a high school student for college? I would begin with a foundational principle as one of our leading indicators: quality over quantity. Does a high school ministry have a hundred kids showing up for "fun" activities, but they are not participating or taking any interest in digging into the Word of God (like Mark's youth ministry)? Or do they have a desire to learn about Jesus and to study with other students? Are they excited to have Bible studies and small groups? Are they interested in sharing with others what they are learning? These are great indicators that youth ministers need to be looking for, and if they are not seeing these types of behaviors emerging, then it should signal a red flag.

Here's the thing. In the corporate world I discovered the old saying "garbage in, garbage out" is spot on. If we don't personally understand why we should have a real relationship with Christ, it will not be genuine. We will go do the "stuff" that looks like spirituality, but it will never be genuine. When people aren't watching we will revert to our old ways, taking shortcuts, dressing the part, and never establishing our own faith. So if you have a youth ministry where students are showing up for the fun events, but they are not showing up for Sunday morning Bible classes, one-on-one studies, evening group Bible studies, or you don't have students calling you to ask Bible questions, then your youth ministry is probably not meeting its primary objective: introducing students to *who* Jesus really is and what Jesus really means for their eternity.

A second leading indicator of a successful youth ministry is what I call relational connectivity. The reason a church should be spending money on activities and events is to hopefully provide robust opportunities to form connections with students. This is the part that may sound contradictory to everything we have just covered, but stay with me. Food is a great draw for any student, especially if it is free. If you are feeding your high school students and not making relational connections with them, you are wasting time and money. You are basically a benevolent operation, and they can get the same thing at the Salvation Army. Your approach needs to be intentional with the specific purpose of forming bonds and relationships. *That* is the purpose of providing food. It is a means to a much more important end. If this is not happening, then your ministry is failing to prepare your high school students for meaningful spiritual development after they leave home.

A third leading indicator of successful youth ministries is conversions. If a youth minister is having a Bible study with an atheist, and they say that they believe Jesus existed, but He is not the Son of God, what is this? How do we classify that person? Have we brought them to Christ? Of course not. From a doctrinal standpoint we need to use the words of Christ as our guide. No one comes to God except through Jesus. There are no alternative routes.

For students to say that as long as they believe in God, and if they are basically a good person, that they will go to heaven is completely incorrect. Where is our Savior in that process? Do we completely negate the cross and the plan of salvation that was the whole purpose behind Jesus descending to earth? That is not what God says. I am shocked to hear how prevalent the thinking is that we can view Christ as a historical figure, a good man, but exclude Him from the salvation process and still secure our eternity!

I hear that dangerous belief system even among churchgoers. The entire Bible is Christ-centered. The Old Testament is preparing the way for the Messiah, the salvation of the world. The New Testament is the fulfillment of this through Jesus Christ. If you have a youth ministry that does not teach this, you are not preparing your student for life after high school.

A fourth leading indicator is youth tracking, not to be confused with stalking. This is tracking that is done post-graduation and is a significant gauge that shows how well the youth ministry accomplished what it set out to do. You may already know that many high school students who "appeared" to be faithful will leave the church once they come to college and will discard their faith background. As youth ministers, it is well worth the time to track the other side of that. How many of your students, after they graduated from high school, sought out a church, were active within a church, and were actively engaged in a good campus ministry? This number is of vital importance and is a number that will give you an objective and accurate snapshot of the effectiveness of your ministry, or lack thereof.

I often wonder why I never hear from youth ministers whose high school kids have come to the university where we have a campus ministry. It is as though once their student graduates, they become someone else's responsibility. I have no praise for this behavior, and if you, as a youth minister, are not following up with all your high school students, you are doing a great disservice to your students. Plus, it sends a strong message to your former students. Trust me, I hear about it almost every day.

The impact that a youth minister has on the long-term spirituality of their students cannot be understated, even after college graduation and beyond. Barna Research and Lifeway have the most recent research on the number of post-college graduates who stay connected to their faith/spiritual development. Their numbers match other research indicating most college graduates between the ages of twenty-two and twenty-nine cease their religious/spiritual activities. The number of college graduates who leave the church ranges from 64–70 percent.

This alarming statistic is no longer causing panic like it once did. In fact, many within the church have grown accustomed to this trend and have resigned themselves to the inevitability of defeat. Initially, the church rallied to address the issue with a variety of responses, some of which were counterproductive and have only exacerbated the problem. The church should not give up because of our failures! We need to refocus our attention and be cognizant of the trending. I have found it helpful to contemplate the issue from a slightly different perspective.

To look at it another way, only 30–36 percent stay faithful. Thirty percent is a low "F" and reminds me of some of my Algebra test scores in high school. Let me ask a serious question: Are we okay with saying that although 70 percent of our kids left their faith, our ministry is successful because 30 percent of our youth who graduated stayed faithful?

Imagine you are an optimist. Going into a surgery, the optimistic person may ask their surgeon, "Don't tell me the odds of dying. What are the odds of surviving?" Even for the optimist, these numbers should shock us like they did in years past. We should feel our stomach lurch in response to a 30 percent survival rate. Those odds are not what anyone wants to hear going into surgery.

But rather than feeling hopeless, we need to get angry! We need to take a good hard look at what we did years ago in response to these numbers and ask, "Why did our response not work, and why in the world are we still doing the same thing, knowing it's not working?"

When I started my work in college ministry, our numbers matched the statistics. But the variables were too many, and my tracking system was not precise. I needed to look at my direct influence-factors that I could track so I could implement an effective plan. Very briefly, because we will discuss the leadership structure later, I believed that part of the issue for our failure revolved around a departure from the biblical model. Christ had a small group of disciples that He taught . . . call it His executive leadership staff. He discipled them, mentored them, and trained them. They then went out and discipled others, who in turn discipled others, and so on.

As youth ministers, striving to have a close and meaningful connection with every student who comes through your door, especially if you have a large group, may be unrealistic and may be stretching your resources to the breaking point. In my case, I began with six college students. Rather than trying to reach every college student myself, I worked closely with these six students, teaching them to teach others. They were my inner circle. I poured into them, and I encouraged them to embrace a sense of responsibility to connect and build meaningful relationships with other students who were their age.

In short, I applied the same methodology we read about in the first century. Jesus gathered a select few whom He worked closely with and they, in turn, went on to disciple others. It made sense to me that for statistical purposes, I needed to track those whom I personally discipled and with whom I spent the most time. I did not realize the far-reaching implications of this simple change. Before I share the numbers, it is important to understand a few simple truths.

First, I will never connect with young people in the same ways that youth will connect to one another. Many youth ministers make the mistake of thinking they have a bigger influence on their youth than the youth have on one another. Part of this is due to the gap in knowledge. Naturally, youth ministers should have a broader and deeper knowledge about doctrinal and spiritual matters than those within their youth program. However, that does not necessarily translate to a relationship wherein the younger person is discipled in a way that establishes deep roots. Yet this is exactly what youth ministers believe. Because they have more knowledge, they assume that they are in the best position to be the primary influencer.

No matter how hard I try to stay relevant with all the college students, the fact remains that I am getting older, and the generational gap continues to grow every year. During my first year as a campus minister, I tried hard to "fit in" with the college students in the way I dressed and the words I used. I wanted them to see me as someone they could relate to, someone who could be accepted into their own peer group. It took me a little over a year to figure out that this came across as disingenuous and desperate.

Fast forward a few years. I was at a college retreat with my group along with hundreds of other college students and campus ministers. I watched as the keynote speakers (all of them in their late thirties or forties) got up on stage to speak. Without exception, every one of them had on skinny jeans, plaid shirts rolled up to their elbows, and tattoos showing on their arms. The look was completed with the sides of their heads shaved close to the scalp and varying degrees of robust Viking beards on their faces. As we closed out one of the sessions, a college student within my group standing next to me tapped me on the arm and said, "I'm glad you don't try to dress like they do. They look ridiculous." It was at that moment I realized an important concept. As ministers it is not our job to try and be another buddy to the youth group members. They have enough people their own age filling that role. What they do need is a person whom they can look up to and provide the wisdom that our age brings to the table.

One more example to drive this point home. I know a middle-aged campus minister whose students have told me that he uses questionable language during his lessons to them. He believes he is connecting by demonstrating his knowledge of the current vernacular. He is trying to show how relevant he is, but what he is actually doing is setting a bad example and driving his students away.

Here is the takeaway: Be yourself and model Christ. Select a few mature-minded Christians within your ministry and disciple them. Be their mentor and not their friend. They have lots of friends but probably not very many mentors. Teach them what it means to be intentional about relationships. Encourage them to develop meaningful relationships with the rest of the youth group. Guide them to the point of understanding how powerfully influential they can be to the other members of their youth group. Then watch in amazement as they bring people their own age to Christ.

As a youth leader, the select few whom you personally disciple should be your focus, not the entire group. Hopefully, it is understood that one is not neglecting all the other aspects of a youth ministry program. There are many elements that must be attended. The advice is focused on relationship building and how one chooses to allocate their limited time and resources. It is incumbent upon the youth minister to judiciously divide up their time in the most productive manner. Hopefully, you are curious to know how this method has worked within our own campus ministry. Theory is good, but what are the actual results?

When I began studying the numbers, I struggled with what my goal should be. Sixty percent retention? Seventy percent retention? Eighty percent seemed way above the average and most likely unattainable. But that was also saying I was okay with 20 percent falling away from Christ. There seemed to be an element of resignation before the battle began, so in the end the only thing that made sense was to set the number at 100 percent. My goal is to have every student whom I personally disciple during their college career remain faithful after they graduate.

At the time of this writing, I have worked closely with fifty-nine student leaders, mentoring, and discipling them over the last decade. The average number of student ambassadors that I have during a school year is between eight and ten. Our average ministry total has ranged from a low of forty to a high of sixty-five.

Unfortunately, I have not succeeded in meeting my 100 percent goal. Out of the fifty-nine student ambassadors who I have discipled, 96 percent has remained faithful. Some will say that this is an astounding success rate based on the national statistics. I recognize this and I am encouraged by the results.

However, it is not something that happens by accident. It requires focused intentionality. There is a level of tenacity and refusing to accept the status quo that must be part of one's mindset. All this said, I would encourage all ministries to set their goal at one hundred percent with the understanding that though the odds are not great, settling for anything less is, in a way, giving up before the battle begins.

To summarize: What are the observable characteristics of a youth ministry doing the job of preparing students for college?

1. *Quality over Quantity.* Are students showing up for the fun stuff, but not growing in their faith? Not coming to Bible studies? Not coming to church or Bible classes? That is a strong indicator that they are there for the wrong reasons and the leadership team is missing the point. Remember, every activity and event should have an intentional purpose. Why are we eating this meal together? Why are we going to this coffee shop? Why are we hosting a Christmas party? To hang out and enjoy some downtime? Okay, but what else? Ask the student leaders these questions.

2. *Relational Connectivity.* If the events/activities/meals being provided do not lead to meaningful relationships, it is a waste of time and resources. Understand that the primary objective for these events is to provide opportunities for your student leaders to engage the rest of the group in meaningful ways. Creating atmospheres that make this natural and easier should be a no-brainer. I know of situations where the money needed to host such events are withheld because those who control the finances view these social gatherings as wasteful. Done correctly, they provide numerous opportunities to invite students to church, invite them to small groups, and initiate one-on-one Bible studies. These events create a comfort zone that is far less intimidating than walking into a church and not knowing anyone or having any meaningful relationships.

3. *Conversions.* If a ministry is not having students declare that Christ is Lord and Savior, something is missing. The above indicators should naturally be leading to deeper relationships, which opens the door for Bible studies. I am a believer in baptism by immersion. I believe it is a necessary part of one's spiritual journey. To put Christ on in baptism should not be an afterthought or simply a symbolic act that

expresses an outward showing of faith. Yes, I realize this is something that is debated among different denominational backgrounds, but put that aside for a moment and explore the deeper question: Why would a person refuse to be baptized if they have accepted Christ as their Savior? In that regard, baptism can be a useful indicator to serve as the point of conversion. In other words, it can be used as an objective data point to gauge the effectiveness of your ministry.

4. *Post-Graduate Faithfulness.* How many of your students are continuing their faith walk after they leave home? It is another indicator that needs to be tracked if a youth ministry program is genuinely interested in evaluating their program objectively. You might be thinking, *What is the point of all this data? A youth minister shouldn't push paper all day, right?* After the system is it set up, it is manageable. This data will provide a compelling picture of the effectiveness (or ineffectiveness) of one's youth ministry. It may be hard to swallow, but let it be a wakeup call that something needs to change.

Youth ministry can be a two-edged sword. The benefits can be vast, but so can the risks. Establishing a Christ-centered youth program in your church requires a great number of intentional discussions . . . discussions that include the pitfalls that we are sharing with you as well as the suggestions.

There are some who will read this book who do not have a youth minister, but your congregation is growing, there are more kids every Sunday, and the parents are beginning to ask about a youth program. What a great problem to have! Also, what a great time and opportunity to start a program off in the right way. Do not assume that parents and church leaders know the risks associated with youth ministry. To them, having a youth minister on staff indicates a growing, thriving congregation that will attract other families, and there is some truth in that.

I advise a cautious approach. Educating parents and church leaders about the potential risks we are addressing will help prevent future issues and will get the program off on the right foot. Please remember that the prize is your child's soul, and Satan is always looking for ways to win. I have found that modern youth ministry is now one of Satan's favorite places to begin his attacks because we have made the pickings very easy. Fixing this issue is not nearly as hard as one might think, but it will require a few dedicated parents as well as a leadership team who will understand the reality of these risk factors, and who are willing to change the paradigm.

2

LEADERSHIP: SPIRITUAL HEALTH OF MEMBERS

We have discussed youth ministry, highlighting some of the pitfalls. In this next section, we pivot our focus to the leadership of the church. As was stated earlier, the church and the home should be in a symbiotic relationship.

I have seen and read many different approaches that churches use to select church leaders. We can read about church leaders in the New Testament. The apostle Paul is clear in his instructions to Timothy in regard to appointing elders within the churches. We know that James and several other apostles served as elders in the church at Jerusalem. We have an abundance of guidance on the qualifications of elders and deacons and the way they should conduct their lives. Our takeaway from this is clear: Jesus expected the church to have leaders who shepherd the congregation. What exactly does that mean? Within this question lies the heart of the problem. This problem has completely changed the way churches across the nation select their leaders and the expectations church members have for their leaders.

First, here is a brief overview of what an elder is supposed to do, according to Scripture. They have a general responsibility to care for and protect the church (Acts 20:28–31), they should be able to teach (1 Timothy 3:2; Titus 1:9), they are to be responsible for the spiritual life of the church (Hebrews 13:17), and they are to be devoted to prayer and the ministry of the Word (Acts 6:2–4).

What do we learn from these passages of Scripture? As Christians, the reasonable observation is that our church elders should be focused *primarily* on the afterlife. They should be immensely concerned about the spiritual health of their congregants above all else. Every one of their responsibilities we read about in Scripture points them to the spiritual well-being of each individual member. With this in mind, we look to the current standard by which churches appoint elders and how those elders interpret their duties.

In doing research for this book, I have pulled from personal histories and participation in church leadership, anecdotal information and observations, and interviews/conversations with past and present elderships from across the Southeast over numerous decades. The results of this study were consistent with my own observations and experience: church elders are nominated and selected based upon their perceived ability to lead others. On the surface that sounds like a very reasonable expectation, but when we begin to dig just a little bit deeper, we must consider how those perceptions by the church membership are formed.

For most, myself included, this character analysis is based upon what we know about a particular individual and their success in the secular world. Almost every elder I have known demonstrated a level of competence and capability in the business world. They have demonstrated their ability to manage money and finances. They dress well and can speak in front of people. They have a likable personality and a degree of charisma. All these characteristics align quite nicely with how the world measures good leadership. It is a foregone conclusion that church members have carried these expectations into the church. One might even argue that it would be odd if church members did not use these characteristics as a measuring stick by which to nominate their leaders. This all sounds good and reasonable, but this is where the problem begins to emerge.

Success in the business world does not necessarily translate to good shepherding, but it appears as though most congregations believe success in the business world absolutely translates to good shepherding. I compiled a list of elders from across the state of Tennessee, including congregations from rural areas as well as urban areas. The list also included a mix of socioeconomic backgrounds and ethnicities. What emerged was a clear picture of church leaders across the state who overwhelmingly shared a few common characteristics. Most of our church leaders are educated (college degrees), hold professional and executive positions, are business owners, and occupy the upper socioeconomic class. In short, they are successful in the business world, and church members believe these are the individuals who are best qualified to lead churches.

When we study the characteristics of Jesus, who is the Great Shepherd, we see a way of leading that may not be viewed as effective in driving profit margins to higher levels. Jesus was humble, submissive, sacrificial, and empathetic. Further, when we look at the men who served as elders in the first century, we find the very opposite dynamic that we see today. These men were poor and uneducated. They were laborers who had physically demanding occupations, and for many of them, they counted success by having enough food to feed their family. We would identify these men today as blue-collar workers.

I need to reiterate that success in the business world does not mean one should not be an elder. At this point, I am drawing attention to what our church membership perceives as a qualified elder. It may be a valid argument to suggest that many worthy men are overlooked or not considered for church leadership because they do not meet our twenty-first-century standards of leadership. In other words, they may not have a college education or even a high school education. They may not be rich. In fact, they may be struggling to make ends meet. They may not own a business or have a fancy title. The best elders I have ever known, men who were wise and cared deeply for the souls of those they led, were poor and without a formal education. They were humble, submissive, esteeming everyone else above themselves, incredibly empathetic, and willing to sacrifice for those in need. Despite their status and income, they demonstrated godly characteristics and their children were also faithful to the Lord. On the flip side I have known some very successful men who were extremely wealthy. As elders, it became problematic for them to esteem others (especially those without education, title, or money) higher than themselves.

Jesus had some thoughts about those who enjoyed success and wealth. None of it was good news. I wish I could offer a simple explanation as to why appropriate, godly shepherding is somewhat of a rarity as one attains wealth or social status. Dave Ramsey is a financial advisor whom I met many years ago at a county fair in Nashville. He had a booth set up and was advertising for his financial services. His financial plan was the product of being bankrupt and discovering some simple methods to attain financial security. Since that humble beginning, Ramsey has grown his net worth to over $200 million dollars, and he has built a thriving financial empire on giving money advice to people who are in debt. I mention him because he is an example of someone whose wealth has not corrupted him based upon his teachings and statements he has made. Consider some of his remarks:

- "Outrageous generosity is the most fun you will ever have with money."[4]
- "You'll never be happy if you chase money and stuff all of your life, but you can find true joy through giving and serving others."[5]
- "Money is a wonderful tool, but it makes a terrible god. Build wealth to use and help others, not to worship."[6]

I really do not want the reader to misunderstand this section of the book. In no way am I saying that wealthy, successful men are doomed to make poor elders. I have known of wealthy men who served as elders, and they were godly leaders. However, based on personal history and the many stories that are shared with me by college students, this is the exception rather than the norm. In my experience, pride is almost always at the heart of the issue. The more one has, the more pride enters the heart. It may be very difficult for a wealthy individual to be deeply attuned and self-aware enough to recognize their prideful ego, and even more difficult to shift their focus from worldly accumulation to spiritual wealth. It could be arrogance. I have been made aware of situations where elders, because of the social status they had attained, believed they were smarter than everyone else. This lack of humility was their downfall and inevitably caused damage to the church.

The number of students I have spoken to who represent hundreds of churches across the country with similar stories has given me cause for alarm. Time and again I hear how churches have split because the leadership is broken and fighting amongst themselves. I believe this has been an issue that has been flying under the radar, so to speak, because most non-denominational churches have a governing structure that is autonomous. In other words, since most non-denominational churches are not connected through a centralized governing body, they are less aware of each individual congregational issue. That is not the case with the large denominational churches. In fact, we know the Methodist church is still struggling for consensus because its leadership cannot agree on the issue of homosexuality. We also know of issues within the Catholic church and their battle within their leadership ranks regarding cases of sexual exploitation of minors. My point is that the lack of information regarding leadership issues within non-denominational churches does not mean issues do not exist. In fact, I would submit that certain leadership issues have become ingrained to the point that congregants either do not recognize the issue or are unwilling to say anything. Further, I would submit that certain leadership issues are so common amongst non-denominational churches that they are not only tolerated but also viewed as conditional characteristics for the leadership. However, it is an issue that is impacting our youth, which is why I am writing about it. Over the next few pages, I will explain how this growing issue with church leadership is negatively impacting our youth.

Issue 1. Church leadership's primary focus is on the physical. The more one thinks about this statement, the more it makes sense. Think about it. If our leadership in churches is composed primarily of successful businessmen, these individuals are hardwired to measure progress through objective measures:

- Is our congregation over budget or under budget?
- Is our facility in good repair or is it falling apart?
- Do we have a growing number of people placing membership?
- Do we have the latest and best worship software with pleasing aesthetics?
- Does our building have curb appeal?
- Are we staying up to date on the trendy coffeehouse type atmospheres within our buildings that will attract the younger crowd?

These are but a few examples.

There is a long list of physical measurement standards that could be listed where it is easy to track progress through tangible, objective standards. These tangible "action items" are easy to display before a congregation. If a church leader can stand before their congregants and demonstrate these physical improvements through graphs, financial reports, and pictures, the message that is communicated is one of competence and outstanding leadership. We love to see results, especially ones that we can experience empirically. So we may have a person in a leadership position who doesn't give a rip about a person's soul, but they sure can bring us a Starbuck-esque vibe to our building and give us a great presentation with pretty graphs!

Before I go further, please understand that I realize the physical elements of church are important and need to be managed. That is not the issue. What I am asking the reader to consider is who needs to manage those physical elements in light of scriptural guidance for our church elders. As I have listened to the hundreds of students who have shared their stories with me, a picture emerges of elderships who are drawn to the work of deacons, leaving the deacons to carry a title as their major job function.

This begs the question: Who is caring for the spiritual needs of the church? When a congregation has no one caring for souls, a door is opened for Satan to hijack the church and take it captive. The effects of this spiritual terrorism can be seen throughout churches across our nation. We begin to see congregations breaking apart, unable to resolve doctrinal differences, discarding a humble spirit and replacing it with a spirit of ungodly arrogance and pride. The building may be in great shape thanks to the management of physical assets, but the souls inside the building are falling apart.

And please understand this: the collateral damage of a leadership team that is disengaged from the spiritual needs of its congregants includes each and every one of your children! Just because they are younger does not mean they are insulated from the message this type of leadership has on their psyche. I have come to view many of the kids who stumble into our college ministry as victims of spiritual PTSD. Demonic bombs are exploding in our churches, and our kids are coming to college with their ears ringing, dazed and confused, with only the smallest shreds of their faith intact.

Issue 2: Church leadership is dominated by apathy. There comes a point in time for every leader where the burden of leadership begins to feel too enormous. We learn early on that trying to find solutions to problems where everyone is content is virtually impossible. Someone is always angry or hurt. Someone is always sowing discord in hopes of undermining your efforts to be a good leader. Society exacerbates the situation by creating postmodernist mindsets amongst your church members so when you take a morally objective stance based on Scripture, your fellow brothers and sisters in Christ shame you and call you intolerant. You may even experience this same ostracization from within your own family. Eventually, the burden becomes overwhelming, and hope is lost. One realizes the battle being fought is pointless, so a spirit of apathy is allowed to have authority, being viewed as the best way to keep peace and avoid constant turmoil.

I'm thinking of Moses as I describe this situation. In Numbers 11:10–15, we get an intimate glimpse of how the pressure of leadership had brought Moses to the point of wanting God to end his life:

> Moses heard the people weeping throughout their clans, everyone at the door of his tent. And the anger of the Lord blazed hotly, and Moses was displeased. Moses said to the Lord, "Why have you dealt ill with your servant? And why have I not found favor in your sight, that you lay the burden of all this people on me? Did I conceive all this people? Did I give them birth, that you should say to me, 'Carry them in your bosom, as a nurse carries a nursing child,' to the land that you swore to give their fathers? Where am I to get meat to give to all this people? For they weep before me and say, 'Give us meat, that we may eat.' I am not able to carry all this people alone; the burden is too heavy for me. If you will treat me like this, kill me at once, if I find favor in your sight, that I may not see my wretchedness."

It is unfortunate that so many people are still reluctant to realize the emotional and mental strain that our church leadership is under. To place the blame of apathy exclusively at the feet of our leadership is unjust. As members who should be submitting to our elders' authority, we have instead created a constant stream of complaints. We have driven our leadership to the brink of despair by our constant in-fighting and bickering. Their apathy is, in part, our fault and we need to own up to the damage we have caused. That said, it is ultimately the individual in the position of leadership that is responsible for their own behavior and their response to outside stressors.

What can be learned from this illustration? First, we see that Moses cried out to God for help and God answered his cry by distributing the weight of responsibility to other men. There is a level of humility that is needed in our church leaders for them to recognize the demands of the job and the limitations of humanity. One of the primary reasons those in church leadership fall victim to apathy is because they feel as though they must do it all or they will be seen as poor leaders. This unrealistic expectation becomes too heavy. Time and again, no matter how hard they are trying, something manages to slip through the cracks. They are juggling a lot of balls, but the church members continue to throw more balls at them until there are too many. It only takes one extra ball to cause all of them to drop. So our leaders stare down at the balls scattered on the ground in dismay and think they have failed yet again. One might think that we would be compassionate to their plight and stop the barrage. But we don't. We continue to throw all our problems and issues at our church leaders, not realizing or caring that their knees are buckling under the weight.

Over the years I have heard church members grumble about the apathy of their leaders: "They don't ever do anything!" "They ignore me!" "Nothing ever changes!" "It is a waste of time to try and get them to do anything!" These accusations may very well be true, but if we stop to consider the bigger picture, we gain a different perspective. How reasonable is it to think that our church leaders entered their position thinking, *One of my goals is to become the best apathetic leader one day!* Sounds ridiculous, right? They begin their leadership responsibilities with hopeful expectations. However, I do not believe that many church leaders realize how pervasive and overwhelming the demands of their congregants will be. In addition to the flood of demands, I doubt that our church leaders realize how rude and aggressive fellow Christians can be either. Together, these two realities can cause even the strongest of our church leaders to give in to despair, and eventually, apathy.

Be that as it may, church leaders must not allow apathy to gain a foothold. Like Moses, when all else has failed, the need to cry out for help is imperative. There is no shame in asking for help when the burden becomes too great. As congregants we need to do better at creating this expectation for our leadership and communicate to them on a regular basis that we support them. In turn, church leadership needs to do a better job in communicating what they are responsible for doing, what deacons are responsible for doing, and what church membership is responsible for doing. The idea of shepherding, as mentioned earlier, is something that many churches do not understand in light of Scripture. Elderships get involved in activities and responsibilities that can and should be handled by others. Congregants burden elderships with issues that should be handled amongst themselves.

I have witnessed disputes and conflicts within the church, but good shepherding is easy to spot when it is on display. It is a leadership filled with grace and godly discernment. It is humble, compassionate, but unwavering in the protection of souls. That means that certain members whose egos are not what they should be will get angry and belligerent when elderships must step in to rebuke so that a soul is protected. The offending member will lash out at the leadership and will try to drum up support to appease their guilty conscious. They will struggle with showing grace and humility. They will find Philippians 2:3 a passage to be disregarded when it becomes inconvenient for them: "Do nothing from selfish ambition or conceit, but in humility count others more significant than yourselves." There is no doubt that these types of people can be found in every congregation and how leadership interacts with them can be challenging. These members are not able, or refuse, to see their own faults and do not realize the peril they are in. Godly shepherding reaches out in grace and love, but it does not compromise truth. Godly shepherding purposes to restore and reconcile relationships.

Why is this important and what is the relevancy of this topic to this book? Because your congregations are telling me a compelling and terrifying story through your kids. They share stories with me of their home churches. If you are a church leader, you need to know that based on the stories I hear, you have not done right by your kids, and I am the recipient of your failure to lead the way God intended. What the youth from your congregation may be afraid to say to their church leaders, parents, or youth ministers, they are freely sharing with me. I hear the good and bad. I hear about the petty drama, divisions, strife and turmoil and I believe it is important for churches to understand that your young people notice these things and are influenced by their home congregations in meaningful ways. Many students have made similar comments to me. "I'm never going back to my home church." This statement carries weighty implications, and it should break your heart. Do not run from the shame these words may cause you. Embrace them and own this reality so you can begin building a better one for the youth who are with you now. There are reasons why your kids are not coming back to your church. Let me share what they are telling me.

First, church has left a bad taste in their mouth. They may have a negative impression of what it means to gather as a group of Christians. Second, your college student has just entered the most perilous time of their life regarding their spirituality. This is the time that you want them at their strongest because they will be bombarded with messages that church is stupid, full of hypocrites, and a waste of time. With all the negative messages about church, faith, and God they will hear from the world, the last thing we want to do is to send them off with these ideas already reinforced. But that is exactly what you have done/are doing. Third, when they begin to contemplate the next step (post-college graduation) this will most likely include a scenario that does not include a church. The exception to this is dependent upon them being exposed to a church while away from home that has their act together. They will need to witness a church that demonstrates what Christian unity looks like and how conflict gets resolved in a biblical manner. Obviously, getting connected to a strong college ministry is important as well.

Hopefully, at this point, the importance of good church leadership and healthy home churches is becoming apparent as we discuss the impact these forces have upon our youth. If not, allow me to share another personal story. Several years ago, there was a young lady who was an active part of our ministry. As the years progressed and she approached her senior year, she was becoming concerned about failed relationships with young men. She was struggling to find a young man who was compatible with her. I learned that she had serious concerns anytime there was a disagreement between her and the person she was dating. These conflicts caused her to question the strength of the relationship, which eventually led to a breakup. One of the root causes for the fear of conflict had to do with her parents. She claimed that they had never had a fight or disagreement all her life. If this is true, one might understand her alarm when a conflict arose within her own relationships. Any married person will admit that conflict and disagreement is part of any relationship.

My guess is that these particular parents decided never to have a disagreement in front of their children. This example paved the way for creating a false picture of the reality of relationships and marriage for their daughter. This girl had no foundation by which to navigate a disagreement with any young man, so she assumed that a disagreement, no matter how slight, meant the relationship was doomed. How unfortunate to create a false picture of marriage for children. By doing this, they robbed their daughter of the chance to witness how conflict gets resolved in a godly marriage, and they provided a completely unrealistic example of relationships.

Children need to see their parents disagree and how parents resolve those disagreements in a Christian manner. (I am speaking in general terms with the understanding that certain marital topics should take place in private). Children also need to know and understand that churches are made up of imperfect people who will not always agree with one another or with church leaders. How those issues are dealt with are extremely important. Some church elders think that every single issue or disagreement within the body of Christ is a matter of national security. Their domain and the discussions that take place within that domain might as well be the holy of holies. What happens within those chambers are only for a select few.

I would argue that there are many smaller issues that can serve as great examples of how church leadership navigates conflict. Yet most congregations try to keep every single conflict, no matter how small, hidden from the eyes of the church. They may be terrified that if the truth gets out the church members will do what? Panic? Leave? Riot? Start a rebellion? All those things?

The point is this: many young people leave home for college with a completely distorted view of church and church leadership. They believe their church is perfect so they will struggle to find another church away from home that measures up. I have had these conversations with some of my college students, wanting to know why they aren't going to a church. Since they can't find one that is "perfect," they stop going altogether, and the habit of not going to church can cause them to fall away permanently. Or they must move back home, limiting their opportunities to disciple in other places. And what happens next? They mature and begin to realize their home church is far from perfect. They become disillusioned and angry and walk away because their home church presented a false picture to them. They discover that their church was untrustworthy.

The other scenario is just as damaging. Some young adults leaving home for the first time know their home church has issues but has no idea how, if, or when those conflicts are resolved. They believe their church leadership is broken and apathetic (perhaps they are) and unwilling to strive for healing. They are glad to be gone and the odds of ever seeing them return are slim.

What is the solution? What must a church and church leadership do to give their young adult a healthy, realistic expectation of church dynamics, including conflict and seasons of dysfunction? To be transparent, my personal experience has been the scenario where all conflicts are kept tightly concealed by the eldership. Again, I feel it is necessary to interject the reminder that I am not referring to the sensitive issues that arise among members that require confidentiality. It should be understood that there are issues that elderships must keep private.

However, logic would indicate that not every single conflict is so sensitive that only the involved parties should know about it.

In fact, I would suggest there are numerous issues that arise within churches that present excellent learning and teaching opportunities for all congregants, children included. These issues provide the leadership a platform to model godly conflict resolution. The benefit of witnessing conflicts within the church being resolved in real time should not be minimized or underestimated. Married couples can benefit by learning techniques to resolve conflicts in the home. Young adults can learn what grace and reconciliation looks like within a body of Christians. The foundation of godly conflict resolution can be demonstrated to the membership allowing them to see that conflicts are part of our human experience and should not be feared or swept under the rug. In fact, members who are open to sharing their stories create an atmosphere for closer relationships and unity within the church. Young adults leave home knowing that no church or relationship is without conflict and that there are healthy ways to move beyond the temporary disagreements between people.

The question now is: How would this actually look within a congregation? First, it must be a paradigm that begins with the eldership. They must have full conviction that the benefits outweigh any perceived obstacles. Second, members need to understand this vision that is communicated by the leadership. Third, a series of coordinated, intentional classes dealing with the topic of conflict resolution should be offered to all the congregation. Class participants should be encouraged to share past examples of their personal experience. These past personal experiences should never be a stage to proclaim the wrongdoing or mishandling of situations. It is possible that some people in the class are still holding on to anger and resentment. All the teachers should be cognizant of certain members derailing the class and using it as their platform to relive old wounds. Because of this potential, every class should set specific ground rules that every member agrees to follow. In this, I advise caution and the use of discernment. You will know your fellow congregants, and it may be that opening up the class to discuss personal testimonies is not a good idea. That is not a problem because there are many biblical examples that make excellent class material offering examples of both good and bad conflict resolutions. Fourth, the minister offers a series of lessons that integrates the class material. Finally, the eldership periodically speaks to the congregation to reinforce their support of godly conflict resolution. In some specific cases, members who have gone through the process of resolving conflict between one another may feel good about having the elders share with the congregants how grace, love, and humility restored their relationship.

The spiritual health of the congregants is influenced by dozens of factors, both internal and external. Our church leadership must recognize the vast impact that spiritual health has on their younger members. It is my belief, based on the many conversations I have had with college students and parents, that unity within the church is a product of the spiritual health and maturity of that congregation's membership. Disunity indicates a lack of spiritual maturity, love, compassion, humility, and grace. Disunity indicates a leadership that may have fallen into apathy.

3

ISOLATIONISM: CONNECTING TO CHURCH COMMUNITY

Done correctly, being a Christian parent today is one of the most difficult jobs you will ever have. I want to stop right here and ask you to reflect on that statement. Maybe read it again. It is not a joke. Christian parenting is *really, really* hard. It will wear you out. I know this because I have tried, and in many instances, failed. Parents who desire to raise their children in a loving, supportive, Christ-centered home are embarking upon a long journey that will be filled with stress, heartache, challenges, and slander not only from those outside the church but also (sadly) from within the church. The support system for parents in many churches appears to be missing.

Yes, I realize that is a broad stroke. Some churches have a great parenting support system, but many do not. Many do not see the need. Many church leaders are hesitant to get deeply involved in the lives of their members. In their defense, many parents do not want their church leaders getting personal with their families. Are you one of those families? What reasons do you have? Lack of trust? How comfortable do you feel going to your preacher or elder and discussing the private issues that are having an impact on your faith?

These are important questions to consider that may be uncomfortable. It could be that your family has always dealt with private matters *privately* . . . within your own family. Understand that when I use the word "dealt" I am not necessarily saying that the result is a good one. Getting help from someone is still seen as a weakness in our society. Church members would rather go talk to a stranger or a counselor they do not know rather than a church leader within their own congregation. What does this say about the unity and connection within a church family? (*Note: Some issues require professional intervention).

This is an area where Satan is wreaking havoc. When we begin to understand his strategy, we can easily see how he is effectively using this approach within the church. Put in simplistic terms, Satan does not like a unified crowd. He is seeking those who are living in relative isolation. He prefers to pick us off one by one.

Consider what James says:

> Is anyone among you suffering? Let him pray. Is anyone cheerful? Let him sing praise. Is anyone among you sick? Let him call for the elders of the church, and let them pray over him, anointing him with oil in the name of the Lord. And the prayer of faith will save the one who is sick, and the Lord will raise him up. And if he has committed sins, he will be forgiven. Therefore, confess your sins to one another and pray for one another, that you may be healed. (James 5:13–16)

Christians are called to rely on one another within the church. They are told to confess their sins to one another. We can say with some level of confidence that this is a rare church culture. This is not how the typical conservative Christian American views life or interacts within their church community. Problems within the home are dealt with privately. We have an attitude that any vulnerability is a sign of weakness. So rather than show our children it is okay to share our brokenness, our failures and our sins with our brothers, sisters, or elders within the church, we show them an example of isolationism.

We talk about this concept frequently within our campus ministry because it is important in taking the fight to Satan. We must understand the tactics he is using for us to take an offensive stance. This concept is easily seen within the animal kingdom. In fact, Peter uses the visual of a prowling lion seeking someone to devour to describe Satan (1 Peter 5:8). We have all seen the documentaries on television that showcase the African safari. We have seen how lions go after the younger animals who are straggling behind. We have also seen the failure of the lion to kill the younger animals in a herd when the herd bands together. This same concept applies to our church family. It is a safeguard that God has given us, yet many families and church leaders discount this protective measure.

Over the past decade I have had parents call to ask if their child is involved in our campus ministry. These are the parents who have recognized an issue, and while they can't quite put their finger on it, they have an intuitive sense that their child is drifting away, straggling beyond the protection of the herd. In almost every case, they are correct. Our campus ministry reaches out to these students, and we make every effort to invite them into our community, but it hardly ever works. Why? The answer is simple. The pattern of isolationism has already been established in this child's life. They are only doing what they have learned to do.

As parents, part of the work you must do at home is to humble yourself. You do not have all the answers. You and your child were created for church community. If you withhold this vital element of how God has created the church, you are doing great harm. When your children see you prioritize non-church events over church gatherings, you teach them that church community is not important—it is non-essential. This leaves an imprint in the child's consciousness when they leave the home.

Also, they will learn that sin and guilt can be resolved in the world rather than in the church, and the world will never resolve sin, only exacerbate it. The first step in unfettering the chains of sin go all the way back to the example parents set at home. There is great power in confessing sin to one another within our church family. We realize we are not alone in our struggles. We discover that many have the same sin issues we do.

As a campus minister and a parent, it becomes frustrating that I am unable to show you the tremendous weight that is lifted from the shoulders of your kids as they learn to lean into each other and their church family. I wish you could see them pray for each other. I wish you could witness the power of healing that comes as they confess their struggles with one another. It builds a union that is stronger than anything the world can give them because it is built upon a principle that Jesus exemplified: humility and submission.

If your children have not seen this at home, why would one expect to see them embrace this type of mentality once they leave the home? The bottom line is this: most parents do not want to lean into their church family for guidance or help because the perception that follows is one of inadequacy. So we teach our kids to pull away, to keep a certain distance from our church family. We become stragglers, and we know all too well how those who are isolated from others fall victim to the world.

Some of the biggest and most concerning issues I am seeing from your young adult children once they reach our ministry are anxiety, depression, and grief. To say these "mental health issues" are pervasive among the college population would be an understatement. It is unusual for a week to pass that I am not talking to a student about anxiety, depression, or grief. Note that I purposely described anxiety, depression, and grief as "mental health issues" because that is the accepted terminology within the university and mental health setting. It is unfortunate that the spiritual dimension is often dismissed, but I will discuss it here for two reasons. First, these issues are rooted in the spiritual realm and connected to isolationism. Second, the seeds of these mental health issues are being planted early on, at home.

In their book, *Embodying Integration*, authors Megan Anna Neff and Mark McMinn discuss the concepts surrounding lamenting, and the human desire to find meaning and contentment despite the difficulties in life. The authors attempt to accomplish this by viewing the search for meaning through the writing of Qoheleth, their presumed writer of the Old Testament book of Ecclesiastes. These authors also discuss mankind being made in God's image (*imago Dei*), and how this might inform our view of self and others within a relational paradigm. As we consider who we are, how we fit into this world, and how our view of God shapes our interactions with others, we discover that humans are intrinsically relational.[7]

This intrinsic need for relational connection is something God planted within our spirit. Nothing about how we were created is meant to be in isolation. God himself is not alone as He exists in relation with God the Son and God the Spirit.

> Two are better than one, because they have a good reward for their toil. For if they fall, one will lift up his fellow. But woe to him who is alone when he falls and has not another to lift him up! Again, if two lie together, they keep warm, but how can one keep warm alone? And though a man might prevail against one who is alone, two will withstand him—a threefold cord is not quickly broken. (Ecclesiastes 4:9–12)

As parents and leaders within the church, we must understand this incredibly important concept and realize how it impacts our children.

I am so saddened to watch student after student enter our ministry having no idea what community is about and what it means to exist in relationship with others. As I write these words, my heart aches for the hundreds of students who are walking collegiate grounds, surrounded by people yet lonely and depressed. These students (your young adult children) are isolated and grieving, and they have no idea why they feel so lonely, sad, and depressed. Why is this happening? Is it possible to model anxiety, depression, and grief at home? Is it possible that parents may be influencing and predisposing their children for future disorders?

The answer to these questions is yes. To understand why, a brief description of the four types of parenting is helpful. Diana Baumrind, a psychologist who worked at the University of California at Berkeley, is credited with identifying these four parenting techniques. They were first described in 1966 and 1967 in two papers that were published. Briefly, they are authoritarian, authoritative, permissive, and uninvolved.[8]

The authoritarian parent has strict rules and boundaries where swift punishment is given to the child who breaks a rule. In these types of homes, children often feel like they are never good enough and will have low self-esteem later in life. The authoritative parent has rules and standards but is open to communication and dialogue when the child breaks a rule. (Experts agree that this is the best parenting model.) Permissive parenting is lenient with few restrictions, which results in children having anxiety issues later in life and are more prone to engage in risky behavior. Finally, uninvolved parenting is the least restrictive. Parents are uninvolved in their child's life. There is minimal communication, and poor decisions and behavior have no consequences for the child. Again, these children grow up with severe anxiety and have a difficult time navigating future relationships.

Would it surprise you to learn that most students I talk to describe their parents as extremely permissive or uninvolved? The first lessons by which a child develops their understanding of relationship and community is through mom and dad. But what happens when parents isolate themselves from their children, are uninvolved, and disengaged in modeling relational living? From my perspective, the results are college students who long for relationships and community but have no idea how to find or recognize what healthy community looks like. They are scared, lonely, anxious, depressed, and grieving. The heart-wrenching part is that they know they are in grief, but they don't know why. Students are unable to pinpoint what is missing, only that something is not right, which leads to further anxiety.

How engaged are you with your children? How have you worked to create community for your child? Do you actively seek out ways in which to model for your child relational living . . . not only at home but also at church? Are you involved in any small groups that include your children, especially as they reach the high school years? Do your high school children have multiple communities and friend groups within their church family?

Answering no to any of these questions should alert you to potential "mental health issues" (spiritual handicaps) that may be present once your child leaves home for college. Lest we forget the context of this discussion, it is this: isolationism puts a human soul at much greater risk. Satan is specifically looking for souls in isolation. As parents, we must model ways for our children to connect with church community, so when they leave home, the natural thing for them to do is connect with church community.

4

TECHNOLOGY: CONNECTING
TO OTHERS

My own children fall into the Gen Z category (1996–2015). Social media was beginning to blossom in the late 90s and early 2000s, but it was not what it is today. Still, when our children became teenagers, we were faced with the decision that all parents inevitably face in our digital world. Do we give in to the tremendous pressure to put the world in our children's hands?

For many parents, the decision was made for them by the educational system. Schools have transitioned from paper books to laptops. Homework is submitted electronically. While many safeguards are put in place, the average teen can easily manipulate these safety measures. Technology moves rapidly and parents do not have the same network capability as a group of teens who are tech savvy and motivated to access the forbidden unknowns of the digital world.

I was torn on whether to share the following personal illustration in this book due to its sensitive nature. In the end, I felt it was right to share because it serves as a powerful example that highlights the point I am hoping each reader will take to heart.

My wife and I had decided to put our two youngest children in a private Christian school due to the issues we knew were taking place in the public school system. Their middle school experience was basically what we expected, but once they reached high school we became very concerned with social media and the internet as they were being manipulated by the students. To our shock, we learned that some students within their peer group had set up a network that allowed females to post nude photos of themselves that could be accessed by other students at school. Even more shocking was the number of girls who were willing to dump their photos into this data file. I am thankful that neither one of our children were involved in this situation, but the ease and expectation for these young girls to get pulled into this situation was alarming.

Please do not be naïve. If your child has access to the internet, then they have looked at or accessed inappropriate material. Not even Christian schools are safe any longer. Are you prepared to fight this battle? If not, I would advise you to get ready and do your research. Your child's soul is dependent on it. I would also advise every church leader to accept what I am saying as fact and start implementing programs at your congregations to address this risk. To the elders and ministers I want to say this: Many of you have willingly buried your head in the sand, and it is past time to own up to what you intuitively know is happening. You know as well as I do that our kids have seen pornographic material and this material is addictive. You also know that it's not just the children. Adult congregants are struggling with sex/pornography addictions.

Would you be surprised to know that most church leaders (elders, pastors, ministers, youth ministers, deacons) struggle with pornography? Psychology Today cites a Barna research study that revealed most pastors (57 percent) and youth pastors (64 percent) admit they have struggled with porn, either currently or in the past.[9] The number continues to increase. If these numbers are accurate, it answers my question as to why so few churches are actively dealing with this epidemic. I believe it is time to move past the shame and to begin speaking openly and honestly about the prevalence of pornography in our churches because it is slaying our youth as well as our adults.

I love working with college students, especially as they reach their final two years of school because of their candid and forthright testimonies. In doing research for this book, I had many hours of conversations with them regarding this topic. They understand social media much better than I do, and their insights into the pitfalls of the digital world have proven invaluable. So, for your enlightenment, I want to share my personal data gathering over the last decade with my college students just in case you still doubt how ubiquitous pornography has become.

- I have yet to interview a college student who has not been exposed to pornography. The vast majority first viewed pornography while still in middle school. One hundred percent of the college students in my campus ministry has been exposed to pornography. *One hundred percent!* This makes me want to scream in frustration and anger! Yet I still talk to parents in some youth groups who believe their kids will never be exposed because they "monitor" their kids' online activity. I have had parents get truly angry at me when I tell them their kid has already seen some type of sexually explicit material. They tell me I don't know what I'm talking about. I have never wished to be more wrong about something in my life. (Parents, it is time for you to wake up! Because Satan and all of hell is awake and working hard to destroy our souls. Yet you are sleeping while Satan is setting your kids ablaze.)
- Well over 90 percent of college students do not view pornography as a "big deal" because almost everyone they know watches or views it from time to time.
- The number of students who talk to me about "porn addiction" has increased every year I have been in campus ministry. From 2012–2021, the increase has been more than 300 percent.
- In the last five years, the prevalence of addiction amongst females has been almost as high as among males.

- Most social media platforms serve as "thirst traps" to entice the viewer to visit other more explicit sites. A "thirst trap" can be defined as a provocative image that does not violate certain media content restrictions that are in place within popular platforms such as Instagram and TikTok. However, the image encourages the viewer to click on a link that takes them outside of that platform and to a site that contains more sexually explicit material.
- Instagram has progressively expanded the filter for inappropriate content. For example, certain nudity is now allowed without filters, and frontal nudity is allowed with only the smallest of filters.
- Snapchat does not filter content. Any images or brief video can be shared within a given community. Again, *any* image or video.
- More platforms are in development that will continue to push content barriers. As easy as it already is to access explicit material, the safer platforms like YouTube are being infiltrated, making it easier for the very youngest populations to view pornographic material.

This is a good time to pause, take a deep breath, and pray for healing. Pray for strength and allow God to use you as a change agent for your church. In the appendix of this book, I have included a variety of resources that deal with this topic. I have spoken to individuals within the ministerial profession who have had addictions, and they have recovered using some of these resources, so there is a good reason for hope because this is a battle that can be won.

However, this is a particular battle that requires a delicate touch. There is a high degree of shame and a real fear of reprisal, especially for those who are employed as clergy or who hold leadership roles. These concerns must be factored in the steps that leadership takes to create not only a compassionate space to confess sin but also a space that is safe from punitive action. Though the percentage of ministers who struggle with pornography addictions is high, only 1 percent feel safe in seeking help within their church. They are afraid of the judgment and the risk of being fired. "This makes sense, because it's hard enough for people in the general population who struggle with sexual or porn-related compulsive behavior to acknowledge the problem, let alone a pastor whose job is to expound on spiritual truths and be a living example of morality above reproach."[10]

I recall a discussion with my parents about raising teens in today's world compared to when they raised me. Although they did not know the extent of policing required to monitor a child's online activity, they did realize it was a potential minefield. They did not envy the lengths to which parents must go today to protect their children from the vast array of material and content available at the click of a button. Unfortunately, the task of creating an atmosphere of normalcy (limited electronics) becomes such a constant battle that many parents slowly acquiesce to the daily bombardment. Simply put, it is exhausting. That is with just one child. Imagine the battle for dominance over electronic devices with multiple children.

As different platforms have begun to captivate and addict our youth across this nation, we are seeing some alarming trends. Suicide rates among young teens have increased. Reports of anxiety and depression among young people have increased. Self-esteem issues have increased while social interaction has declined. Our kids are more connected (electronically) than at any other time in human history but more disconnected (face to face) than ever before. More concerning, the reported use of social media apps (Facebook, Instagram, Snapchat, etc.) is growing exponentially among older demographics. Kids are seeing their parents disengaging from them, which is exacerbating the children's feelings of isolation and loneliness. Relational living within the home has, in many cases, ceased to exist as a result of our iPhone and laptops. Screens have taken the place of parents.

As I discussed in the previous section regarding parenting styles, how sad is it that we are living in an age where a screen can so captivate a parent that it literally changes how we would otherwise parent a child? Perhaps as you were reading through the parenting styles you identified with one more than the other. Most parents would like to claim that they are the authoritative parent, but in reality they are permissive or uninvolved. Christian parents are not immune, and I would suggest that most do not even realize that they may have drifted to one extreme as their time shifts from relational living to electronic living.

Adam Alter, a professor at New York University said in his book *Irresistible: The Rise of Addictive Technology and the Business of Keeping Us Hooked* that Steve Jobs, the inventor of the iPad, never let his kids use one. Jobs was quoted after being asked about his kids loving the iPad, "Actually, we don't allow the iPad in the home. We think it's too dangerous for them in effect."[11]

At this point it should be a forgone conclusion that screen addiction is real. There are so many good research articles that have been written on this topic that citing them here seems to be pointless. We all know what is happening . . . has happened. The issue is not that we are now living in this strange reality, but what have parents and churches done to address it?

As was mentioned earlier, we have seen evidence that some churches saw the need for a support system that deals specifically with this issue, but most churches do not. In many cases, parents are now on the screen as much, if not more, than their children. It is a self-feeding, self-perpetuating cycle that is creating an atmosphere in our homes that is hungry for the world and not Christ. Bible studies with our kids have been replaced by Netflix. Time around the dinner table with the family is not so common anymore. (As you will read later, eating food with our children and family is actually a vital spiritual act that has a lasting impact.)

So what is the work that needs to be taking place in the home? And how does this work impact the youth program at a church, the church at large, future involvement with a college ministry, and finally, a young adult who is now eager to put down roots in a church rather than boots to walk away from it all? In the next few pages, we will discuss the major elements that are vital in cultivating a healthy spiritual landscape for your child and the mindset that every parent must adopt to stack the odds in favor of Jesus and connecting to others.

WEEDING OUT THE WORLD

The only way we get out of this world is to die. According to the apostle Paul, dying was something he desperately looked forward to because he would be gaining the kingdom and the rewards of heaven. However, Paul also recognized that while he was living in fleshly form in this world, he still had the opportunity to proclaim Christ to the lost (Philippians 1:21). The task we all face while occupying this brief physical existence is how to keep the weeds of the world from reaching the point of prohibiting our growth. More importantly, how do we manage the weeds while simultaneously bringing others to Christ?

The answer is simple, but the execution is hard. Hard, but not impossible. Like anything worth doing, it takes a certain level of dedicated intentionality. What we are really talking about here is what I call replacement therapy. Taking something out of our lives and replacing it with something else. This is hard for us to do in the twenty-first century because we have so many things that can take the place of more important things. In fact, I would argue that this is much harder to do in today's world than it was in the first century, particularly the Acts 2 church community. So I want to ground this section within that paradigm.

Here is how Luke describes that early church community:

And they devoted themselves to the apostles' teaching and the fellowship, to the breaking of bread and the prayers. And awe came upon every soul, and many wonders and signs were being done through the apostles. And all who believed were together and had all things in common. And they were selling their possessions and belongings and distributing the proceeds to all, as any had need. And day by day, attending the temple together and breaking bread in their homes, they received their food with glad and generous hearts, praising God and having favor with all people. And the Lord added to their number day by day those who were being saved. (Acts 2: 42–47)

Perhaps it is superficial of me, but the part of these verses that strikes me is all the eating that was taking place. These were people who loved to get together and eat.

What is it about sitting down with another person or group of people and enjoying a meal together? It was a while before I learned that most of our college students hardly ever sat down with their family to eat a meal. They were too busy with homework, ballgames, practices, band, and a plethora of other activities. Parents had to work late. Siblings had to be shuttled around. Errands had to be run. Doctor and dentist appointments were scheduled, elderly parents needed care, and the list goes on. By the time everyone was home together, it was close to bedtime. The last thing on anyone's mind was sitting down at the dinner table.

Add to this hectic schedule the distractions of social media, television, movies, gaming, etc. Not that any of these activities are inherently bad, but they have replaced a special way in which families connect. The idea of a family sitting around the dinner table and eating a meal together seems like a scene from bygone years, a faded memory of the past. Family meals are seen as an option that might happen once in a great while but are not a necessity. I would argue the opposite. Eating together is vital in so many ways. It is one of the primary vehicles that allows a family to connect with one another.

I believe that God designed our bodies in a way that we are to enjoy food and to enjoy it with others, in community. It brings us together in a shared experience. It breaks down barriers and promotes conversation and relationship building. Sitting down and eating together forces us to step out of the business of life and to reflect on more important matters. Friendships are built and strengthened over a meal. People fall in love with each other on dates in a nice restaurant. The holiday memories that sustain us and bring warmth to our souls are often occasions that occur around the table. Some of my fondest and funniest memories of my grandparents happened while we ate a holiday meal together.

I spoke of intentionality. Family meals don't happen anymore because we are not intentional with making them happen. The expectation that everyone is at home to eat together is viewed as completely unrealistic. The burden may fall on your mother or wife, and if she is working, how can she prepare a meal? Is a family supposed to deny their children the opportunity to be in band, sports, theater, or other activities just so they can eat together?

There is no doubt that the hectic pace of life in today's world creates plenty of obstacles, which is why I believe the first-century church may have had a little easier time in this regard. That said, it is a universal truth that we make time for things that we view as critical. In fact, if we are being honest, we make time for things that we want to do that are not critical. We somehow manage to find the time to watch that show on Netflix. We somehow find the time to browse the internet, post our political rants and vacation pictures, tweet random thoughts on Twitter, maintain our Snapchat streaks, get sucked into TikTok for hours, and rearrange our schedule so we can catch the newest Marvel movie. Yet we find it nearly impossible to sit down at the dinner table and eat a meal together.

At our campus ministry, most of our events are centered around a meal. Before we have a devo, we eat. Before we have our midweek Bible study, we eat. Before we have worship on Sundays, there are donuts. Almost all our monthly events involve a meal. I am intentional about us coming together on a daily basis and eating together with one another. Why? Simply stated, it is what they did in the first-century church, and God added to their numbers. I don't have any science to quote, but I can tell you that God has added to our numbers in amazing ways.

I believe that this is because one of the cornerstones of our ministry involves us frequently eating meals together.

Regarding families, I would highly encourage you to take some electronic activity out of your busy schedule and replace it with a meal. As I was growing up, my family was as busy as any family one might see today, apart from the social media distractions. Both parents had jobs and my two siblings and I were involved in about every extracurricular activity available to us. However, my parents made it a priority for us to be at the dinner table at 6:00 p.m. every night. Granted, there were times when we could not do this, but these missed family meals were the exception. Our dinner was a sacred time for us. It was how we connected as a family. Although I may not have appreciated the significance of these meals while in high school, once I was in college they served as a bedrock and anchor during difficult times.

I have not put all the pieces together in my head yet, but I know God had something in mind when He created us with the need to eat and when He blessed us with tastebuds to enjoy food. Think about that for a moment. He could have created us without the need for food if He had wanted. If you have not done so already, I would recommend reflecting on the numerous examples in Scripture where we see the importance of building fellowship, fostering community, and reconciling ourselves to God while eating a meal together. From the provision of manna, to covenant meals with the elders of Israel, to the times when Jesus reclined at the table with sinners, tax collectors, and harlots, to the Passover meal, we find food serving multiple roles.

Sustenance for the body and soul, the table invites us into community and opens avenues to unified fellowship. It is well worth our time to understand this concept and to begin training our children in the art of dining with family and friends. Let us strive to substitute the wasted time we spend in secret staring at a screen with time at the table.

5

MORAL RELATIVISM: CONNECTING TO CHRIST

Paul begins 2 Timothy 4 by telling Timothy to be ready to preach the word at all times and to do so as a way of reproving, rebuking, and exhorting, with complete patience and teaching. Paul then goes on to explain that this is to be done because a time is coming when people will not endure sound teaching. Rather, they will seek out people who will teach things that match their own passions, and they will turn away from the truth and wander off into myths. We know that before the first century even came to a close, distortions had infiltrated the church. Consider Paul's word to the Galatian church:

> I am astonished that you are so quickly deserting him who called you in the grace of Christ and are turning to a different gospel-not that there is another one, but there are some who trouble you and want to distort the gospel of Christ. But even if we or an angel from heaven should preach to you a gospel contrary to the one we preached to you, let him be accursed. (Galatians 1:6–8)

As the centuries have passed, mankind has seen thousands of new religions that are completely contrary to the gospel of Christ that was taught by Jesus and his apostles. These variations to God's Word were all born from secular desires instead of God's will. I have often wondered how it is that through every age of man, societal "norms" can have such a strong influence on the doctrinal truths given to us by Christ. True, humans are a fickle bunch, easily persuaded and impacted by the society in which we live. Most people are so entrenched in their secular world views that no amount of teaching will persuade them to consider a different perspective. This has become especially concerning in our current age and its understanding of morality.

For example, a recent conversation I had with a college student went something like this:

"What gives you the authority to tell someone what they are doing is wrong?"

My reply, "God's Word."

"And how is it that we should be expected to live by a flawed book that is over two thousand years old?"

"First, it is not flawed, but that is another discussion. Second, God is the one who dictated how we are to live, and I believe He is the moral authority in all things, not man or any given society. There are absolute truths by which we are to live our lives."

"Well, I don't believe that. I believe God wants us to be happy. I believe that what you call absolute truth can't be applied to all people for all time. That is ridiculous. Your truth may be your truth, but my truth may look completely different. Your position is absurd and intolerant, and that is not a Christian concept."

"So you're saying I should be more tolerant?"

"Yes!"

"Why?"

"Because it's the right thing to do!"

"So you're saying there is an absolute truth based on right or wrong? That tolerance for others is universally good?"

At this point in the conversation the student realized she had been backed into a corner and tried to begin backtracking her statements with exceptions and special circumstances.

We spoke at length about morality and truth, but she refused to concede that God superseded what our current society, social media, the entertainment industry, and her university professors (to name a few influencers) were telling her. In fact, she was so strongly convinced that my position represented the uniformed and bigoted position that she was willing to abandon logic to maintain her position. In the end, it was my conclusion that her influencers had so strongly prejudiced her worldview that she found moral absolutes truly offensive. Sadly, she represents a growing number of college students who feel the same way. I would argue that this societal drift into relativistic morality poses a very real and serious threat to our children at every stage of development. There are several reasons why we need to be aware of what is happening in our world today.

First, moral absolutes have become offensive to our society. Moral absolutes are viewed as antiquated and legalistic. Tolerance is strangling the life out of moral objectivity, and many are eager to witness its demise.

Second, the lines between what is morally good and inherently wrong are being obscured by Satan and his influence in our society today. Gone are the days when good and evil were clearly recognized. Everyone knew that Luke and the Rebel Alliance were the good guys, and Darth Vader and the Imperial forces were evil. This is not a picture of our world today. The lines between good and evil have become increasingly obfuscated.

Third, tolerance is fantastically subtle. It masquerades as the darling of goodness while winking deviously at the evil lurking just outside the door. I'm not saying that tolerance is inherently evil. I am saying that we have allowed it to grow into something grotesque and massively pervasive. It has become a god of sorts, and society is expected to bow down to its every whim, the good and bad alike. Issues that were once defined (objectively) as wrong are viewed by the world today as acceptable. In extreme situations, what was good is now evil and what was once evil is good. Prophetically, Isaiah 5:20 alerts us to this fact. This disturbing transition is taking place in every facet of our culture. Tolerance demands *not just* the acceptance of things that were once clearly seen and identified as sinful behavior, but it also demands the approval of these actions.

Fourth, this mindset is finding its way into Christian homes, Christian universities, and churches. Highly educated and intelligent people who stood firm on many basic tenants of scripture have gradually changed their position. We need to understand why once devout Christians no longer agree with various biblical passages that call certain lifestyles and actions sinful.

I recently read a blog by a minister who preaches for a church in middle Tennessee. He has applied a postmodern hermeneutic to Scripture that allows him and his congregants to justify the sin of homosexuality. The reasoning that is used to support their position requires a very deep dive into textual criticism and the original Greek language. Their reasons to justify homosexuality using new interpretations have been summarily dealt with, and no serious biblical scholar can maintain a position that the Bible endorses or accepts homosexuality as permissible, but few are willing to pursue these scholarly rebuttals.

Instead, our children are being convinced by cleverly phrased arguments as they sit in churches across our nation and are taught a perverted version of the gospel, albeit an acceptable, tolerant, and postmodern version. If that is happening within churches, what do you suppose is being taught in our secular universities? And this is but one example. Tolerance is the vehicle by which these agendas are being promulgated upon our children, and it is cleverly packaged within the context that Jesus was all about love and acceptance. And although that is true, it is only part of the story.

Fifth, the proponents of subjective morality argue that true Christianity must be viewed through a lens of tolerance, and the doctrine of grace is used to support this convincing argument. The issue is not what churches (and some religious universities) are teaching about Jesus is wrong. Rather, the teaching is incomplete. You see, Jesus never loved someone to hell. And that is the danger in taking an otherwise godly concept (tolerance) and applying it carte blanche to all our

interactions with mankind. The marriage of grace and tolerance is pol-
luting the gospel.

A brief divergence on the concept of grace is needed at this point, so
allow a moment of explanation. The Greek word used for "grace" in our
Bible is *charis*. New Testament writers understood the concept of *charis*
in a different way than we do. For us, grace is something that is freely given (correct) given in abundance (correct) and something that we
did not earn or deserve (also correct). However, most of us have been
taught that grace is given without expectation for us to do anything in
return. (There are numerous theological views as to how we arrived at
this conclusion, but for the sake of brevity, we will just accept the fact
that this is how many understand grace.)

For the New Testament writers, they understood grace to be something that required the recipient of grace to pay back—much like taking out a loan from the bank and paying back that loan over time. You
might see how this goes against what we have been taught regarding
grace. Our inspired writers of the New Testament also understood that
the gift of grace that God gave us was impossible to pay back. It was a
priceless gift that only our Creator could give. Even so, the expectation
was that we would respond in a way that demonstrated our heartfelt
gratefulness, which should lead the Christian to a powerful and genuine effort to do the work, to bear our cross, and to seek the lost.

This attitude of gratitude makes it impossible for us to have a sense
of entitlement. The overwhelming value of God's gift to us should, in
effect, wreck us. It utterly breaks us when we realize the significance
that grace has in our eternal position. Our obvious response, as children of God, is to do everything in our power to show him the gift is
not lost on us. It should compel us and motivate us to work diligently and with burning intensity for God's kingdom because of the hope
that He gives us.

This concept is important in understanding how postmodern
thinking has utilized the collective worldview to create a monster and
represents the danger when tolerance (not love) becomes the god of our

age. So, coming full circle, we need to be reminded about the woman who was caught in the act of adultery (John 8). Jesus did love her beyond words, but He did not shower her with grace only to walk away and leave her with an entitled mindset. He did not leave her to think that her value system was morally good based only on her desire to be happy, no matter her lifestyle. Jesus left no room for argument when He told her to "sin no more." He recognized her actions as sinful, and He called her on it. He never said, "I love you so much and would never want you to be unhappy. And since I am abundant in my love and grace for you, I will tolerate your lifestyle."

Yet that is exactly the logic that postmodernists are applying in our churches today. In essence, they are telling people that living a lifestyle of sin, as long as it is a loving relationship, is perfectly fine. In fact, what is sin? Who are we to say to someone they are sinning since morality is subjective? If someone wants to practice homosexuality, that is okay. If someone wants to get divorced for any reason, that is fine. If someone thinks it is okay to sleep around on their spouse, we need not lecture them on the danger of being separated from God by this sin. We must accept them for who they are and love them to the point that our love will somehow exonerate them from their sin, even though they have no plans to stop. After all, God wants us to be happy because he created Christianity, and as Christians, we must be tolerant.

Let me be very clear on something. That *is not* loving someone. That is condoning an action that is clearly defined in the Bible as sinful, and if you are sitting back quietly not warning people (in compassion and love) that they are putting their eternal souls in jeopardy, then I would call your intentional lack of confrontation an act of evil. We are living in a world where offending someone is considered worse than the sin in which they are ensnared. Did Jesus offend people? Absolutely. Many got so offended by His words they couldn't stand to be around Him, so they left, disgusted and angry.

The great apologist C. S. Lewis wrote a brilliant piece regarding something he called "chronological snobbery."[12] It is the idea that we accept, without critique or analysis, any new way of thinking because it is new. We toss out the old simply because it is old, and we do not see it as relevant any longer. Progressive Biblical scholars believe that there are new and better ways to interpret Scripture. A younger generation of theologians have gone to prestigious seminary schools to learn these new interpretive standards. This new hermeneutic is lauded with much intellectual snobbery to be appreciated by the sophisticated theological student.

Here's the truth: boil all these new buzzwords down to their core and one is left with a pathetic excuse to justify man's teachings and not our Lord's. These are the same excuses men have tried to use through the ages. We have just repackaged them into intelligent-sounding words and have deluded ourselves into thinking we now somehow possess a greater understanding of Scripture. Just stop and think about the absurdity of that for a moment. Think about the towering arrogance that one must have to assume this generation is somehow gifted in Scripture that we can use the Bible against itself.

My point is to bring some awareness to the destruction of moral absolutes. The Bible and its foundational tenets are systematically being eradicated because they are considered too harsh, unloving, intolerant, and divisive. And the vehicle that is effectively bringing this into reality is tolerance. We are calling it love, but it is a devilish sort of love that ultimately will bring about the soul's destruction. So be judgmental when it is needed. Be intolerant. Love your brother or sister enough to tell them if their soul is in jeopardy. They may get hurt and angry, but that beats the alternative.

To tether ourselves to this new mode of Christian thinking only untethers us from Christ and His teaching. We attach ourselves to the ever-changing fickleness of whatever time in society we find ourselves. For parents, it is imperative that you recognize what is happening at the university level and guard against this teaching in the home (and unfortunately, even some churches) because it is disconnecting our youth from Christ. There is another aspect of subjective morality that I have seen gain traction in the last decade of working with college students, especially as the church continues to emerge from the height of the COVID pandemic. The argument basically diminishes the need to be part of an organized religion. The reason given, as I often hear it phrased, is, "I'm a spiritual person, but I'm not really into the whole organized religion thing."

The argument goes something like this: "I believe in God and Jesus, but I don't think we should waste time and money going to church. Instead, we should focus on 'being Jesus' to those around us all the time. I'm not really doing this when I go sit in a pew several times each week. I can do good by spending time with those in need . . . like homeless people, or sick people." Certainly, this person's heart is in the right place. We *do* need to "be Jesus" to all those around us who are in need. Further, it is easy to look at "organized religion" today and get a bad taste in one's mouth. The vast amount of money and resources being poured out so that our church members keep coming back and giving more money can be obscene. Where does all that money go anyway? To the homeless? To the widows? To the hungry? Perhaps. Or maybe it is going to something else like stage equipment, bands, entertainment, lights, lasers, and hefty salaries to the hip motivational speaker. For many, it is hard to reconcile the expense that organized religion is willing to pay to engage, captivate, and retain their church members—to keep them coming back for more.

Jesus Christ wants us to be spiritual, and He also intends for us to be religious, which means active in our worship and church attendance. His original plan had us fellowshipping with each other (that is, with other church members who had accepted Him as their Savior) as often as possible. In fact, we get an incredible blueprint of how things were supposed to be in Acts 2. And the Hebrew writer reminds us that we should not neglect gathering with our church family in Hebrews 10. Some of our first-century brothers and sisters in Christ had grown complacent (just like us) in attending church service.

Here is what Hebrews 10:23–25 says:

> Let us hold fast the confession of our hope without wavering,
> for he who promised is faithful. And let us consider how to stir
> up one another to love and good works; *not* neglecting to meet
> *together*, as is the habit of some is, but encouraging one another,
> and all the more as you see the Day drawing near.

The reason given by the Hebrew writer for gathering and not skipping out on our assemblies is so we might provoke each other to love and good works and to exhort one another. This is the very thing that the "spiritual but not religious" person says we should be doing. Our motivation to go out in the world and do these good things begins in church.

Let's be real for just a second. You know as well as I do that if you are out there alone trying to do something, it gets really hard. In most cases, you are going to give up. Everything that is worth accomplishing gets accomplished because other people are pushing you to keep going, encouraging you, and motivating you. We build and grow off each other. We become better people because others are challenging us to become better people. That's one of the reasons why we go to church. Not because we are perfect and have it all together, but because we are broken and need each other.

Some who read this may believe that going once on Sunday morning fulfills their obligatory church attendance requirement. I think they may be missing something much more important and something that will have eternal consequences. When we give up the opportunity to provoke each other to love, good works, and exhorting each other, we are, in essence, saying that we don't need the church (as a unified body . . . a body that each member has a specific part to play). We are diminishing the body as a whole because we are withholding our own unique abilities that are meant to "stir up one another to love and good works . . . encouraging one another." We are failing to connect to Christ.

So I'm left wondering: How many Christians who decide to skip church are out there working with the hungry and homeless during those worship hours, or just lying around at home watching television, doing laundry, or sleeping? Understand why Christians go to church. Worshiping God, provoking me to love and good works, and exhorting me will never be a waste of your time. You may, in fact, be helping me and others like me connect to my Savior in meaningful ways and, ultimately, that helps me get to heaven.

Unfortunately, many who claim to be Christians are saying that going to church is not a necessary function and to make church attendance a moral issue is not only misguided but also a false teaching. As I reflect on this new attack from within the church as well as outside the church, I marvel at the creativity and craftiness of Satan. How better to isolate us even further than to interfere with the gathering of the saints?

Satan was not sitting around idle while COVID impacted our physical world. On the contrary, he capitalized on this epidemic with astounding speed and aggression. In essence, our enemy was able to shut churches down across the nation, and many churches had to close for good. The trickle back into worship services has been slow. Thousands of former members never came back, and remember, church attendance was already at an all-time low. Maybe this does not alarm you. If not, at least be alarmed by the evidence of a supernatural being who can orchestrate such a massive shift in our collective thinking in a matter of two years and successfully impact our connection not only to each other, but also to Christ.

PART 2

THE SPOKES

I heard an analogy a long time ago about how our interpretation and application of God's Word is like a human body with a skeletal system that serves as a structural component holding everything else in place. Everything else includes our skin, blood, organs, etc. The analogy goes on to explain that all the laws and commandments are the skeleton while the skin, blood, and organs represent concepts such as love, grace, mercy, compassion, faith, and so on. If, as Christians, we are only focused on the legalistic issues and matters of doctrine, all we present to the world is a skeleton, which is scary. And if we are only focused on love and grace and mercy, all we are is a glob of bloody skin and organs (also terrifying). Obviously, we need to be proportional in our application of God's Word because both parts are vital to our salvation.

I share this because the wagon wheel I am using as an analogy is similar. I have proposed the concepts in section one that I believe to be the outer structure of the wheel, giving it form and purpose. In this next section I will be discussing the spokes that provide the outer wheel with strength and support. These spokes also serve to connect the concepts of the outer wheel to the wheel's hub. One might even suggest that the spokes provide pathways to the hub.

6

TAKING INVENTORY

What does it mean to take inventory? Take inventory of what? And why is this relevant to our discussion? The years I spent in the executive world taught me that most people and organizations tend to tackle projects without taking the time to prepare and count the costs beforehand. I love this passage of Scripture that highlights the foolishness of doing just this:

> For which of you, desiring to build a tower, does not first sit down and count the cost, whether he has enough to complete it? Otherwise, when he has laid a foundation and is not able to finish, all who see it begin to mock him, saying, "This man began to build and was not able to finish." Or what king, going out to encounter another king in war, will not sit down first and deliberate whether he is able with ten thousand to meet him who come against him with twenty thousand? And if not, while the other is yet a great way off, he sends a delegation and asks for terms of peace. So therefore, any one of you who does not renounce all that he has cannot be my disciple. (Luke 14:28–33)

So what are we taking inventory of and how is this done? Years ago, I worked with a person who had been part of an elite military unit in the army. We would talk about survival tactics, and I was always fascinated with the level of training he had to endure. One of the topics of conversation between us was what a person needed to do in survival situations, and he said one of the first things a soldier needed to do was to take inventory.

I asked, "Take inventory of what?"

He said situational awareness was vital, and a good soldier was able to inventory everything around him. Location came first. Was he in a safe space or did he need to immediately move to a different location? Once he was secure, he took inventory of his surroundings to see if anything could be used for his survival needs. Then the soldier would inventory his personal assets. What supplies did he have on his body or in his gear, assuming it was still with him? There were many other things he shared, but these two items have always stuck with me, and I think they are a good analogy for this topic.

Looking at the first step, the soldier immediately examines his location to determine whether relocating is needed. As Christians, one of the most important activities we can do is to constantly examine our location, spiritually speaking. Stagnation, as I have seen, is a battle we all must fight. We tend to settle in and get comfortable. Some of the hardest workers I have ever seen for the Lord's church have fallen victim to stagnation. Their location is no longer safe. Our church leaders are not immune to this danger either. Congregations can become stagnant to the point that everything they do is nothing more than going through the motions. They might look alive from the outside, but inside they are dead. I wonder how many churches are just like the church in Sardis that Jesus rebuked:

> And to the angel of the church in Sardis write: The words of him who has the seven spirits of God and the seven stars. I know your works. You have the reputation of being alive, but you are dead. Wake up, and strengthen what remains and is about to die, for I have not found your works complete in the sight of my God. (Revelation 3:1–2)

As a church leader, do you look around your congregation and wonder why so few are willing to volunteer their time outside of worship? As a parent, are you disappointed by church leadership's complacency? As a youth minister, are you concerned that your youth group doesn't engage any longer in lessons or activities? As a preacher, are you seeing more of the church members' excitement for the Lord fading? In short, are you in a church that is just going through the motions of Christianity? If any of this sounds familiar, your location is susceptible to attack. You are in a bad location and if you stay in the same spot, you will die.

Let me be clear: I'm not suggesting that everyone suddenly leaves their church and goes searching for a new one. That is the last resort. Instead, changing location should be viewed from a spiritual standpoint. I have witnessed amazing transformations within congregations when just one person or just one family decides to move their spiritual location from a place of stagnation to a place of rejuvenation. Change may be slow in coming, but it will always be worth the effort. The problem arises when no one is willing to be the first person to reignite the fire and passion. Reasons for this vary from one church culture to the next, but the underlying cause remains the same; churches have allowed a spirit of idleness to take root.

Be forewarned, the person or individuals who startle people out of their stupor will have to endure pushback and opposition. One of the hardest things to do is to get something started again once it has stopped moving. It takes an enormous amount of energy and effort, but once it starts to move, continued movement becomes much easier. That is why so many churches remain stagnant. It is too hard to get them moving again, and for the person doing the pushing, the resistance directed at them becomes especially difficult.

I am sure everyone has heard someone say, "We've always done it this way." As I mentioned earlier, C. S. Lewis coined the phrase "chronological snobbery" to describe people who wish to change traditional ways for newer ways only for the reason that the old ways were old—it matters not whether change is needed. This is not what I am talking about here. What I am saying is the change that is needed in situations where "the way it has always been done" was never the right way to begin. Perhaps this is the reason why the church stopped moving, doing, and renewing in the first place. This is Physics 101. Objects in motion tend to stay in motion while objects at rest stay at rest. It is time to ask yourself, *Is my church, and my location, in motion or at rest?*

The work of taking inventory, be it at the group level or the individual level, is no easy task. In essence, we are stepping into the role of judge, and this work does not end until a sentence is passed down. That is a daunting task and the reason why so few people endeavor to do it.

The college students in our ministry, representing dozens upon dozens of churches across the states, are part of a generation who do not understand, nor do they connect with a church whose words do not match their actions. Not that this generation is perfect, but what they have in abundance is a strong desire to serve. They are a "doing" generation. They are not content to sit in a church and listen to sermons about serving others while the church makes no effort to actually go into the community and serve.

In fact, the concept of authenticity continues to come up in the research as to why college students have stopped going to church. When I ask college students what are the biggest reasons they don't go to church, I hear the same answers. In contrast to the graph that I shared in the opening of this book that showed the decline in church membership in adults, the below graph indicates the decline in church attendance specifically among college students.

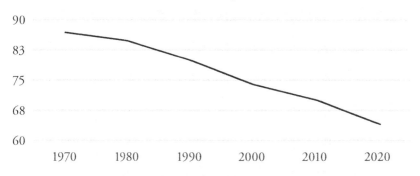

Attendance at Religious Services

This data is collected from the CIRP Freshman Survey, which has surveyed a large sample of entering college freshmen students since 1966.

Part of the work in taking inventory is to study and understand what is taking place among our college students. Do churches understand that this is the primary pool from which future church members will come? Collectively, the church needs to be cognizant of how social changes are impacting the spiritual perception of our young adults. We are clearly living in a time when social justice is resonating within the college age population. Churches who are rejecting this mindset because of political leanings are cutting off their own legs. Understanding the college students' current belief system is different than agreeing with their belief system, and this is an important distinction.

Is it possible that the line in the sand that was drawn by churches back in the 1950s did not anticipate a postmodern world that has so captivated our youth? If we are not willing to walk over that line and reclaim our youth, the consequences of this reticence will be devasting to the Lord's church. Walking over this line does not mean we are changing church doctrine! What it means is that we become open to the idea that the approach that attracted and held college students almost a century ago may not be the best approach to use today. As one can see, taking inventory might mean doing some hard work and making tough decisions to evaluate one's location, assess whether one is stagnant or in motion, and then doing the hard work of making needed changes.

Taking inventory includes another area that is often neglected: identifying assets. At the risk of sounding overly dramatic, I think one of the most heartbreaking issues within the church is unrecognized and ignored talents. Part of responsible church leadership involves the ability to identify talents within the membership and effectively utilize those assets. In most cases, members are excited to offer up their talents for kingdom work. In some cases, talents must be teased out and encouraged. I challenge the reader to look at congregations that are thriving. A common theme among these thriving churches is a leadership who has not only identified the talents of its members but has also matched these talents with impactful ministries. There is an expectation by the members of these churches that their talents will be used and their unique, God-given talents are afforded the opportunity to blossom and grow.

Amazing things begin to happen in this type of environment. Members will begin to experience a connection to God in powerful ways. They will be empowered to explore the spectacular depths of God's unique gift to them and how their specific talents are meant to be used for the glory of God. A few (very few) of my college students have come from such congregations and let me tell you how incredible it is for me to watch them as they live out their Christianity for others to see. It is powerful! When these students cycle through our ministry, the draw they have is manifested in amazing stories of salvation, restoration, reconciliation, and redemption.

It may sound like an exaggeration, but I believe that if every church provided an environment that enabled its members to unleash the power of their talents, and their children were exposed to this type of system throughout their years at church, the impact at the collegiate level would be felt across our nation. Professors trying to push moral relativism onto their students would not be met with the passivity we witness today. The pushback against subjective morality and subjective truth would create a modern-day education revolution. Not only that, but the impact on our society would be immediate also. The world would be turned upside down and Christianity would have an opportunity to thrive as it did during the apostolic age.

I'll be the first to admit that I'm a dreamer. However, I've seen the power and influence that just one student has when they have been raised in a church that empowers the unique talents that God has given each one of us. I believe the suppression and stifling of those talents not only damages the church, but it also has a repugnant stench in the heavenly realm. There is something distinctively soul-damaging when a man, woman, or child sits in a church year after year and their talents have been hindered or discouraged.

Imagine if this were the position you were in. You became a member of a church with excitement and high expectation that the church would encourage you to utilize your talents for God. But as the years passed, you were never asked about your skills, or worse, you offered your skills and were repeatedly told they do not need help in those areas. Eventually, you learned that it is easier to remain quiet. The only expectation the church had for you was to show up on Sundays and give your money.

How would this affect your attitude at home, or at work? Do you think your kids would come away with a feeling of hope and anticipation that their talents would one day be engaged in meaningful ways? Or would they begin their collegiate journey believing that Christianity is nothing more than punching a clock and going through motions wherein their expected contribution is to fill a pew? Our collective talents are meant to be used not only as a way to present Christ to the world but also as a way of serving each other.

The apostle Peter wrote:

As each has received a gift, use it to serve one another, as good stewards of God's varied grace: whoever speaks, as one who speaks oracles of God; whoever serves, as one who serves by the strength that God supplies—in order that in everything God may be glorified through Jesus Christ. To him belong glory and dominion forever and ever. Amen. (1 Peter 4:10–11)

Taking inventory is crucial. As congregations existing in a postmodern world where our college students are being fed a diet of subjective truths, we must wake up from our stupor. We must take an honest look at where we (and our church) have come to rest. Is it a good place or a dangerous place? Is it moving or stagnant? Do we need to be a change agent? Are we prepared for the pushback, and if not, what needs to happen to prepare ourselves? Finally, we must begin the work of establishing environments where our talents will be identified and used for the Lord's church.

7

BUILDING A TEAM

Inasmuch as a single individual can be the catalyst for change, continuous improvement and sustaining an environment for growth is a group effort. It requires a dedicated team. Consider the following two passages as we discuss what it means to build a team:

- "Iron sharpens iron, and one man sharpens another" (Proverbs 27:17).
- "For the body does not consist of one member but of many. If the foot should say, 'Because I am not a hand, I do not belong to the body,' that would not make it any less a part of the body. And if the ear should say, 'Because I am not an eye, I do not belong to the body,' that would not make it any less a part of the body" (1 Corinthians 12:14–16).

When I first started my role as a college minister, I knew I wanted to surround myself with college students who shared my passion for reaching out to other college students. I mistakenly thought that my role needed to be equal to or greater than the students who would be leaders at our student center. I imagined myself walking the campus, talking to students, inviting them to our ministry. It didn't take me long to realize that this was not an effective strategy for two primary reasons. One, I'm older than they are, and it freaks them out to have an older male strike up a conversation. Two, social interaction has changed dramatically since I was in college thanks to our digital lifestyles. Face-to-face interaction is infinitely more complex and requires a certain navigational skill set that I did not possess, nor do I possess now.

This is the new world in which we live where social, face-to-face interaction has devolved into a strange ritual as a result of social media immersion. This immersion into the digital world has left our youth highly inexperienced in face-to-face meetings. Talking to strangers is so far out of their comfort zone that I have witnessed more than a few college students have legitimate panic attacks.

Finding a leadership team that has been raised to look people in the eye, shake their hand, and maneuver themselves through a series of pleasant verbal exchanges is becoming more difficult. I even had to modify my own approach with students because I came across as too abrupt and intimidating because my focus on another person's eyes made them uncomfortable. Developing a team needs to take into account the social dynamics within a given environment. For example, I know that my specific target audience is college-aged students, so I need to develop a team whose members are knowledgeable with this demographic. The more unfamiliar one's team is with a given group, the harder it becomes to train the team. I share this simply as a precursor for thinking about how a team might come together. Assuming that a team has been selected, I would like to offer a few suggestions on training them.

There are five major fundamentals that I use to train our student ambassadors. These five principles are: Create empowerment through delegation, learn through teaching, expect excellence and give praise, be patient while holding the leadership accountable, and lead by example.

1. *Create empowerment through delegation.* I can't tell you how many times I have become frustrated watching one of our student leaders fumble through a task, making obvious mistakes, and basically creating more issues for me to fix. I must fight the urge to step in and do it myself. If you are constantly compensating for your team members because you know you can do a better job, you might as well not have

a team. The point is to give them the freedom to make mistakes and when they do, take the time to sit down with them and suggest another way, and then let them try again, and again, and again . . . until they get it right. And trust me, they will eventually get it right. In fact, sometimes they will surprise you and find a better way than how you would do it! This takes time, but by empowering them, you create a dynamic of competency that will pay massive dividends long term.

2. *Learn through teaching.* One of the biggest pushbacks I get as a college minister is our students *not* wanting to get up in front of others to lead various projects, speak, teach, or conduct a Bible study, etc. But I tell them that the best way to *truly* learn something is to teach it. If you know that you are expected to stand in front of a group and teach them about the characteristics of the early church as we read in Acts 2, odds are you will spend some time reading and researching Acts 2. You will think about potential questions. You will think about applications. In short, you don't want to stand up in front of people looking unprepared. Creating a cohesive and functioning team involves giving them opportunities to lead. The more they do it, the more comfortable they will be at it, and some will even discover they have a talent and passion for it.

3. *Expect excellence and give praise.* What do you get if you only expect mediocrity? If your answer is "mediocrity," you are wrong. By nature, people will hit just below your minimum expectations. *Hey, why work hard for something if I don't have to?* We all do this, whether we care to admit it or not. We take shortcuts even when we know it might not be wise. I do it myself. Standing on a ladder, cleaning out gutters, reaching further and further when what I should do is get down off the ladder, move it over, and climb back up. Instead, I overextend, wanting to get the job done faster.

Our students are no different. If you are thinking that you want to be realistic and in doing so you set your expectations a little lower than what you might have, expect to get something lower than what you expect. Instead, expect excellence. Talk about it in your team meetings.

Discuss how the last event or retreat could have been better. After most retreats I give the students who attended a survey asking them to grade us on how we (the leadership team) did and how we can improve our next retreat. Everyone knows that I set my expectations high for myself and for our student leaders, so they strive to do their best.

High expectations should be balanced with healthy amounts of praise for jobs well done. I learned an interesting thing in the corporate world, and I wish I could remember the source, but it is long gone. In a nutshell, the study found that if you give equal praise and equal criticism, people will say that they received 80 percent critique and only 20 percent praise. If you give 80 percent praise and 20 percent criticism, people will say that you gave praise and criticism in equal measure! The point is to praise often and loudly. Make it a big deal, especially if you must critique.

4. *Be patient and hold your team accountable.* I don't mind telling you that one of the most repeated requests that I ask of God is more patience. I would love to be able to tell you that working for the church and running a college ministry is nothing but sunshine and flowers, all day, every day. Some days leave me reeling because I had a student tell me something that I know will impact their life forever. Sometimes students that I have poured into with everything I have will disappoint me in ways that are hard to describe.

Also, team members can become like family. Your emotional investment in them is tremendous, as it should be. With that investment comes vulnerability. Striving for godly patience in these times is tough, and practicing wisdom and constraint can be equally hard. Knowing when to say something is as important as how you say it. Galatians 6:1 speaks of rebuking someone in gentleness.

One of the first things we do as a team during the summer before the fall semester starts is have a leadership retreat. During this retreat we talk about expectations and accountability. I even have each leader sign a "contract" that outlines the expectations. It is a tool that reminds them that I will hold them accountable for certain things, but more importantly it is a tool that helps them hold themselves accountable. Everyone will make a mistake from time to time. As leaders who are striving to model Christ, we should be gracious toward the members of our team in times of shortcoming, but we must also address the shortcoming. To ignore the issue is to accept the issue, which is not something we should do.

5. *Lead by example.* Finally, here is the tough one. If we are going to talk the talk, we must walk the walk. Nothing will destroy our credibility faster than doing things that we would not want our team to do. As leaders, whether it be in a secular job or a leader in the church, community, or in a college ministry, if you are not willing to serve while you lead, the willingness of those who follow will always be reserved. They will hold back to some degree. That doesn't make a person a bad leader, but it also does not make them a great leader. And given the choice to be good or great, we should choose great. John 13 is where we see our Savior demonstrating servant leadership. I encourage any new team to read this passage.

The other crucial part of building a team is not as tangible. I'm introducing the reader now to a very specific corporate phrase. The business world is full of these little catchphrases that get overused and repeated to the point of nausea. Like these catchphrases, those of you who have worked in the business sector will be familiar with "stakeholders" and "buy-in." I dislike these phrases as much as the rest, but in this particular setting they are relevant and fit well with what I want to explain.

Stakeholders. In an organizational setting, the term "stakeholder" is meant to describe those individuals who are the primary decision makers. They are the ones with the most capital invested in the company (usually). It stands to reason that within any group, one will find stakeholders. In my personal situation as a campus minister, I have five different groups of stakeholders. First is the eldership of the church that is our primary sponsor. Second is the church members at that same sponsoring congregation. Third are the other sponsoring churches. Fourth are the students at the college ministry itself. And fifth are the private donors/alumni who help support our work.

That is a *big* list of stakeholders, so hopefully you can appreciate the complexity of understanding the needs and expectations of each group, which creates some navigational difficulties. The hard part is trying to reconcile the different expectations of each group, especially when there is a conflict of interest. The way in which I handle this is to prioritize my stakeholders. For me, these are the stakeholders who have direct oversight of the ministry. I do not want to minimize the importance of the other stakeholders. In a perfect scenario, all the stakeholders appreciate and understand the importance of one another. As one of the ingredients to a successful college ministry, church, or organization—one that will thrive and grow—this must be part of your strategy planning, and the team must understand the relevance of each group.

Buy-in. This term is used to describe the emotional connectivity of the stakeholders to their investment and the programs and principle-operating philosophies that drive that organization toward its primary goals and objectives. In other words, you must convince your stakeholders that your ministry is needed, effective, and impactful. They need to be emotionally connected to what you are trying to accomplish, and this can only be done through effective communication. You need to stay on their radar screen, so to speak. Share what is going on with your ministry, share the conversion stories and testimonies, invite them to your dinners, devotionals, and retreats. Involve them as much as you can, but within reason.

I realize that talking about stakeholders and buy-in is not exciting. Some might even question why it would be included as a part of a primary spoke. Years ago, my wife and I decided we needed to build an addition to our house. The first few months didn't seem like any progress was being made. The area had to be cleared out and then a footing had to be dug and concrete poured into the footing prepping for the foundation blocks to be set. As the weeks went by, it seemed like the actual structure and framework would never begin. That was the exciting part, and we were anxious to see what the actual house would look like once the framework was done.

This spoke is much like the prep work and footing for a house. It must not be ignored, and organizational leaders need to realize that skipping this step will lead to catastrophic failure in the future. If we don't understand the expectations of our stakeholders, and we begin implementing programs and outreach ministries without taking the time to plan, issues will arise and some of them will be serious.

Let me give you another example from a corporate perspective. I was working as a liaison between DuPont and its contracted workforce, tasked with developing a training program that would integrate contract employees working beside DuPont employees. This was a tough issue because the two work groups did not get along. The contractors were viewed in a negative light because they were coming into "DuPont territory" and working for much less money. DuPont employees felt threatened that their jobs would be taken away if the contractors demonstrated competency.

The crux of the problem was the DuPont employees were expected to train their contract employee counterparts, and needless to say the training from the DuPont employees was counterproductive. I was expected to fix the problem. The training program I developed was solid. But I had two stakeholders whose investment needed to be understood. I also knew that if I didn't create buy-in from both groups, it didn't matter how good my program was. It was doomed to fail.

Despite my eagerness to get started with the "meat" of the training, I realized the necessity to have foundational work before beginning. I met with every employee in both groups to understand their concerns, needs, and expectations. I asked them how they would approach the situation and how they would suggest training. I then met with the leaders of each group together to discuss and share the concerns. Finally, we brought both groups together to have a planning session where we identified all the reasons to make it work and the consequences of competing with each other.

Some were still skeptical, but I had created enough buy-in from the group leaders that the outliers fell into place. Remarkably, the suggestions and plans they expressed were almost identical to the plan I had developed. So instead of a new guy bursting into their workspace saying, "Things are going to change today, and I have a training program that I expect everyone to follow," both teams together created an atmosphere where concerns were addressed, and they felt like they were part of the change. They became invested because it wasn't just my idea. It was their idea too.

The same principle can be applied to church ministries, and this illustrates why knowing your stakeholders and creating buy-in will reduce issues. It is foundational work that cannot be ignored if you expect long-term positive results that are sustainable.

8

ENGAGING IN ACTIVITIES

The reality of the situation is that events and activities are necessary and play a key role in developing relationships in the home, church, and ministries. Activities can also be a detriment to relationships if done incorrectly. I want to spend this chapter talking about the importance of activities as well as their inherent problems.

We should begin with a few premises, and I will focus on campus ministry for illustrations, though these principles are easily applied in a variety of different group settings. First, money is necessary to buy food and fund activities. Second, most people enjoy getting together to enjoy a meal, especially when it is free or costs very little. Third, people have an abundance of choices regarding how they will spend their time. Fourth, the family, church, or ministry is constantly competing against the activities the world is offering. In the college setting, these other activities are especially compelling due to the social expectations within this demographic. If we are to have any hope of competing with the plethora of distractions, it is imperative that we get busy and develop a plan that offers varied activities that will attract people and keep them coming back for more.

Which brings us back to a few of our premises. Money and the appeal (and necessity) of food. On the surface this seems to be an easy enough task to accomplish, but it can be daunting if you have not planned. To begin, someone must pay for the food, which means a food budget is required. Knowing how much, when, where and what to feed groups must be planned and organized. Food is expensive and wasting it is . . . well, wasteful.

For cost considerations, there are options where families may be able to help so the entire amount of purchasing a meal (especially if the group is large) can be distributed among numerous people. An obvious example is the typical potluck meal where each family brings in a dish. A strategy I use at our campus ministry is to have a free dinner and devotional once every week during the school year. If one time per month a sponsoring church brings in a meal, that helps us tremendously with our food budget. The weekly dinner and devotionals have become a major part of our ministry and one of our most important activities, but it must be thought out and planned to be impactful.

I mentioned earlier about meals and eating together at a table. I cannot emphasize enough how important this simple activity can be. It should not be surprising that Jesus used meals as a way of teaching and connecting with His disciples. Some of the most important discussions took place over a meal.

We purposefully have a devotional after our meal because we have found that more people are likely to stay if we feed them first. Having a devotional first and then eating is a mistake. People will just show up late for the food. As an activity, this is one that can and should lead to further Bible studies. Devotional topics should be timely, relevant, and thought- provoking, which means they can't be thrown together at the last minute. I speak at most of the devotionals in the fall semester, and I use the spring semester to give our student leaders a chance to develop their speaking skills. The college students respond well to seeing their peers stepping up to offer Biblical instruction and teaching. Our students also enjoy singing. We provide PowerPoint slides with the words to the songs and have several students lead our singing before our devotional thoughts are presented. This is a simple, pure, and uplifting form of praise and worship that has always resonated well with our students.

None of this is easy work. The takeaway is that this seemingly simple activity takes a lot of planning and preparation. Done well, it will

bring in students who at first will come for the meal but will later realize the devotional that follows the meal is something they have been
craving too.

Twice every week during the school year we provide a lunch for
all students, faculty, and staff. This is a meal that we charge a nominal
fee to help cover the cost of food. We have another meal on Wednesday nights before our midweek college Bible study. And we obviously
eat meals on our retreats. The main takeaway is that we use meals as
more than just a belly-filling activity. Students come to the table and
talk, laugh, get to know one another, build bonds, and form relationships. On Tuesday nights one almost needs some earplugs because the
laughter and conversation can be so loud. Meals bring people together.
Many students have come back after graduating and have told me that
some of their fondest memories at our ministry were the meals. It can
be a powerful thing and should be an integral part of any ministry or
outreach effort.

Welcome Week begins the Thursday before classes start in the fall.
At the University of Tennessee at Chattanooga, almost every student
organization has a blitzkrieg of activities, starting with freshman moving in on Thursday through the following Saturday.

In the summer, I bring my leadership together for a retreat, and we
take hours to plan our Welcome Week activities. Every day and evening we host an event for new and returning students. Cookouts, pic-
nics, hikes, movie and game night, karaoke contests, capture the flag,
scavenger hunts, etc. Each activity must be carefully planned and led
by our student leaders. (Social media plays a huge part in getting the
word out, so having a person who is tech savvy is helpful.)

These events are all about meeting as many people as possible and
getting them into our facility to see that we are a viable option to all
the other non-religious organizations that are not interested in saving
souls. It is an exhausting week and one that requires a great deal from
our student leaders. Most universities do something similar, and this
is one of the best opportunities to make new students feel welcomed

and comfortable with the college ministry. One of the highlights of this week is our Welcome Sunday where the students will be exposed to our home congregation, our college class, and a big fellowship meal after our morning worship.

You may be reading this and wondering how any of this applies to your situation if you are not leading a campus ministry. *How does what I am sharing apply to a home or church environment where these types of outreach opportunities are not available?* First, I believe it is important for parents, youth ministers, and church leaders to get a picture of what campus ministry looks like and how we integrate spirituality into campus life daily. And not just any campus ministry, but our campus ministry. The reason is because our campus ministry is successful. By design and intentional effort, we have developed a program that is beating the odds, as was mentioned earlier in this book.

Looking at the statistics across campus ministries, the vast majority are falling away during their college years. Our ministry is retaining 96 percent post-college, and these students are becoming active members in the Lord's church. If you care about soul saving, outreach, and church growth, that number should get your attention. That said, if I'm a parent, youth minister, or church member/leader, I would be looking at this and wondering how to apply these methods within my own contextual environment.

Different church leaders, members, and parents have asked about our ministry over the years, and I have gladly shared what we are doing. In almost every conversation they will say something like, "Yeah, that would be great if logistically we could do the same thing in our home or church or ministry." On one hand I understand the unique advantage we have as a campus ministry. We have a great space for students to hang out all day. We have a budget that allows us to spend money on food for them. We have a staff that plans and organizes events. We serve a population who, for the most part, are not tied down to jobs or careers that support families. They have the time and freedom to "do life" at our ministry. We are also in a very convenient location. We have access to students because our facility is right next to the campus. It seems impossible that this set up could be duplicated in any other setting, except maybe another campus ministry. If that is what you are thinking, you have already admitted defeat. I will be the first to admit that duplicating this system can be difficult in a church or home setting, but difficult is not impossible.

As COVID started shutting down churches, including our student center, it gave me a real opportunity to put my money where my mouth was, so to speak. If I had to take the most important element away from our student center, the one thing we do that has the most impact on our students, it would be small groups.

So while churches were closing, we pivoted ever so slightly and started a variety of small groups wherever we could. I began one at our church as well as in in our home on Sunday nights. We started Zoom groups. I began a podcast to keep everyone plugged in. I would say those who participated are closer now to one another than before COVID emerged. Fellowship, food, and the study of Scripture. Sharing our lives with one another. Despite the ups and downs of churches opening and closing, restricting services and numbers, social distancing and mask mandates, our small groups thrived.

I truly believe that this is a testament to the importance of maintaining our fellowship in any way possible. In fact, it opened our eyes to a better way of relating to one another and ultimately to the strengthening of our faith in Christ Jesus. And if another shutdown happens, we are ready.

What about at home? How can this be done within the busy lifestyles of families? Allow me to be blunt. Jesus is either your priority or He is not. Fathers and husbands need to do what God commanded us to do and lead our families spiritually. That means creating an environment at home where spiritual matters are talked about openly and frequently. For some families, this might require a set schedule of devotional time. For other families, this could look like fellowship around the dinner table—whatever works for your family's schedule.

But without intentionality, you know as well as I that it won't happen. The original small group was the family.

It is possible to duplicate the most important element that we do as a ministry, and this is one of the primary reasons why we experience the numbers that we do. But what about churches? Well, that one requires a slightly different approach. Let me jump back to our ministry for a moment and share another important activity.

Retreats. Our college ministry has a fall retreat and spring retreat. I have discovered a few very important facts about retreats. First, if I can get a new student to attend a fall retreat (which we schedule as soon as we can in the school year—usually in September), the odds of them sticking with our college ministry is high (over 80 percent). Second, our retreats take the students out of their normal settings and gives them a unique opportunity to bond in ways that are not possible on the college campus. Third, I put a great deal of effort in finding speakers who will connect and resonate with the students and offer thought-provoking lessons. Fourth, it allows me to have lots of one-on-one conversations and Bible studies with students and develop meaningful relationships. They get to see a side of me that is harder to show during the normal school year.

I have experimented with several different retreat formats, and here is the one that has worked best. We have three sessions that mirror our weekly devotionals. First, we sing hymns, then our speaker presents a lesson, after which the students break up into small discussion groups for a period of time. After the small group discussions, we reconvene as a large group to process the breakout sessions. The speaker usual-ly facilitates the large group discussions. I try to limit each session to around two hours.

Months before the retreat I will have numerous meetings with the speaker to share the topic I would like covered, the types of questions that can be used for the small groups, and many other details about how the weekend will progress. We have found a facility that is large enough to accommodate a sizable group, has an industrial kitchen, a massive open space for our devotionals, and plenty of tables to eat our meals. There is also lots of outdoor space for games.

Congregations need to have retreats for their members. Retreats promote growth and closeness with other members. Retreats are an incredible way for Christians to reignite their faith and passion for Christ. Consider the opportunities for intense small groups to develop over a weekend. I can think of no reason why church leaders would not be able to provide this type of opportunity. Granted, it requires careful planning, which is why I spoke of developing teams in the previous chapter. Planning a retreat is definitely a team activity, so the cohesiveness and diversity of a team who would put an activity like this together is crucial. Also, seriously consider bringing in an outside speaker who is respected and trusted rather than using paid church staff or the minister. These individuals need a break too, and this is a great time when your preacher and staff can receive much needed spiritual nourishment.

Monthly Events. We try to have one event per month where students can come together and enjoy one another's company. The events do not have to be complex or cost a lot of money. What we are building when we do things like this is a sense of belonging, a sense of bonded community. We are building a family atmosphere, and for some students this is a new experience. Without activities none of this would be possible. I realize that many churches are good about having events. Some have regular potlucks or fellowship meals once every month, and others do game nights and plan outings as a congregation. All of these are great ways to connect, so why do churches still struggle with a sense of unity and closeness? A couple of reasons come to mind.

First, and for many congregations, the events have become stale. The once per month fellowship luncheon after the worship service is so ingrained as a tradition that the meal has lost its real meaning. Does anyone get up and speak about how significant it is to be eating a meal together with their brothers and sisters in Christ? Would this be an odd thing to happen if a person stood up at your next fellowship meal to share their feelings? Do churches cultivate that kind of openness and vulnerability anymore? I do not think it would be a stretch to say that if something like that happened, it might completely change the entire vibe of the fellowship meal. The staleness, I think, would immediately dissipate and something significant might begin to happen. Sometimes, we just need to be reminded. Sometimes our comfort zones need to be invaded.

Second, churches need to become way more intentional about how its members interact and relate to one another. This is where intergenerational meetings should happen. Why is it that only the older members have a say in fellowship events and opportunities? Would it be so bad to include younger individuals? They might have some incredible and refreshing ideas. These are just two suggestions that I believe can have an immediate impact on getting the most out of your church or home relationship building activities.

Some may say that you don't need to do "stuff" to have a relationship with another person. My response would be for them to come to a university and try to build a relationship with someone without first doing something with them, whether inviting them to go grab a cup of coffee or to a free dinner. It is an argument that is not based on reality.

Think about it. What meaningful relationship have you ever had where you did not do things together? Whether it is a spouse, coworker, or relative, there needs to be something that brings the two people together at a particular time and place that leads to discussion. At least in the beginning stages. Once two people know each other well and have found common interests perhaps they can decide to go sit under a tree and talk. Otherwise, suggesting to a person you have just met that you would like to go sit under and tree and talk to them is a good way to end a relationship before it begins.

Here's an anecdotal example. The minister at the congregation I attend wanted to talk with me during the COVID shutdown. Our church and student center were closed so he suggested we meet in the parking lot of a Sam's Club. We both brought chairs and coffee and talked for two hours to get caught up (social distancing being properly observed). My point is that we were at the point in our relationship where this was not weird, but we only got to this point because of the many activities that he and I had been part of in the past.

That said, social norms need to guide us, and today's college student will be much more likely to respond to overtures of friendship if they are integrated into an activity of sorts. We have found a great deal of success by using group activities to form relationships. I would argue this principle applies across the board.

9

DEVELOPING RELATIONSHIPS

As I discussed in the last chapter, without activities, developing relationships would be very difficult. I want you to consider your relationships with people right now, and think about how you would classify your relationships by using the below picture:[13]

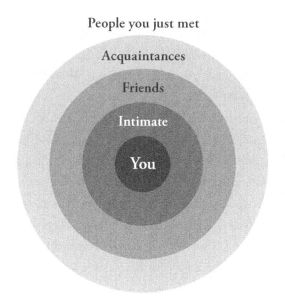

We cannot be intimate with every person we meet. An intimate relationship takes a tremendous amount of work and time. When we look at the biblical model of relationships, it is a fantastic guide for us to follow. In fact, I use this as the only model for our college ministry. Jesus selected a small group that He spent a great deal of time with. He ate with them, He instructed them on a daily basis, and He poured into them more deeply and intimately than He did with others. This is the first circle that is closest to you.

Also, notice the color of the circles. The more intimate the relationship, the closer in color the circles are, but the further out they go, the less the colors are the same. This represents the level of influence one has over another individual. It makes sense. The closer one is to another person, the higher degree of influence. I have an intimate relationship with my immediate family, and they have a great degree of influence over me and the decisions I make, how I act, and what I do.

In Matthew 28:19–20 we can observe the intimate relationship that Jesus maintained with His apostles. Consider His words closely: "Go therefore and make disciples of all nations, baptizing them in the name of the Father, and of the Son and of the Holy Spirit, teaching them to observe all that I have commanded you." These are not words that would be used on acquaintances. Maybe not even friends.

These intimate relationships are the most impactful. It is where real change occurs, where real dialogue takes place, where the difficult, soul-searching questions are asked. As a college minister, one of the primary functions is to develop deep, meaningful, impactful relationships with the students. But not all of them. Again, using the model that Christ established, He only selected a few. And I would submit to you that even among the twelve apostles, He had ones whom He was closer to than others. Circles within circles. I would imagine that His relationship with Peter, James, and John was on a different level than that of Philip, Judas, or Thomas, although that is pure speculation on my part.

Meaningful relationships take time and effort. It can be messy and sometimes unpleasant. Some of the closest relationships I have had with my student leaders have also been the most tumultuous. But real change cannot take place with superficial relationships. In the resource section of this book, I have included a list of questions. These questions are meant to be a guide for you. They are an illustration of what meaningful questions look like and the types of questions that can only be asked once a relationship has reached a certain level. If you do not feel comfortable asking these questions to a person within your close sphere of influence, something is amiss. If you are looking to develop leaders and you are serving as their mentor, you *need* to be at a place in your relationship where these questions can be asked.

I realize that I'm stating the obvious, but we all need to be reminded that developing relationships is an intentional endeavor. Deep, impactful, life-changing relationships do not happen by accident. They take deliberate thinking. You must ask, *Where do I want this relationship to be in six months, one year, five years?* Then you must work to develop that vision of what could be into what is. I think the church at large does not have a great deal of these types of relationships because they make a person vulnerable to a degree, and nobody enjoys putting themselves into a vulnerable position. We do not want other people to know our struggles, our sins, the things that prevent us from reaching our spiritual potential. So we stay in a place of self-imposed isolation, never developing any meaningful relationships that challenge us, motivate us, and encourage us. This is nothing new.

In the 1960s, Chuck Lucas, the campus minister at the Crossroads Church of Christ observed these issues. He reasoned that this lack of genuine closeness and unity was a hinderance in bringing people to Christ. Relationships were viewed as weak and superficial. People would come to church, sit in a pew, and leave without making any real connections. And all of this was true. In fact, I would argue that for many churches this same dynamic is still prevalent. Christians can see this. They can recognize that it does not match the familial vibe that we read about in Acts as Luke describes the early church Christians and their relational connections to one another (Acts 2).

So Lucas started what would later be called the Crossroads Movement, which would lead to the Boston Movement, and from the Boston Movement, the International Church of Christ (ICOC) was born. During his ministry, Chuck Lucas converted a young man by the name of Kip McKean, who later called thirty disciples to be totally committed to Christ. In 1979, this small group of students would later plant one of the fastest growing churches, the Boston church of Christ, and this church later became the epicenter for the discipling movement. In 1988, the Crossroads church of Christ disassociated itself from this movement, and in the 1990s the ICOC formally split from the mainline churches of Christ.[14]

Their intention was good. They recognized the lack of genuine relationships as an obstacle for real change and growth. They wanted to make a few very close connections and be disciples to those few, who would then in turn disciple others, akin to the relational model that Jesus used. This group experienced rapid growth and many people thought they had found a way to reintroduce a relational model that closely resembled the early church. The "thing" that was missing within congregations seemed to have been found again, and thousands were experiencing a way of doing church that filled a void. However, events took a turn. The mentors (disciplers) began to use personal information that had been told to them in confidence by the people they were mentoring. An element of coerciveness and control entered the relationships. When individuals wanted to sever ties, they were told that their secrets—their personal sins and struggles—could and would be used to bring them back into line.

Being vulnerable to another person requires trust. In this situation, trust was broken, abused, and mishandled. As a result, the benefits that might have come from this movement were overshadowed by the harm it caused to people and families. In fact, I would suggest that it created a new foundational belief where many different denominational backgrounds became apprehensive and reluctant to pursue anything that resembled this type of approach. I can only speak to my own personal experience, but what I have observed in my life has been a refusal by church leadership to promote any kind of program that encourages mentorship. I would even go so far as to say that any programs that even hinted at mentorship or discipleship became anathema to many faith-based organizations, primarily because of some bad players. The proverbial baby was tossed out with the bath water. To proclaim oneself as a "disciple of Christ," or even worse, to say that you were being "discipled," was tantamount to a confession of cultish lunacy. In fact, many conservative non-denominational churches are still averse to using the word "disciple" because of the historical baggage the term recalls.

So where does this leave us? Hopefully, it leaves us with lessons learned and a new way forward. I cannot see any reason why church leadership should not be able to reexamine and employ past approaches that had stunning success while filtering out the issues that led to apostasy. Developing relationships with another person should never be for personal gain or for the building up of self-ego and pride. As Christians, any relationship with another human being should have, as its primary goal, the intent to share the story of Jesus in a genuine and meaningful way, motivated out of compassion and love.

This brings us to the real takeaway. What I mean by this is that we need to be working on our relationships to the point where it makes perfect sense to discuss the four points below. Not just talking about them for the sake of talking, but also speaking about them with purpose and passion.

1. *Proclaim Jesus is Lord and Messiah.* "So let everyone in Israel know for certain that God has made this Jesus, whom you crucified, to be both Lord and Messiah!" (Acts 2:36). This will never happen if you are not intentionally working to develop a *real* relationship with someone. And if this is true, how in the world can you talk to someone about repentance without a meaningful relationship (Luke 13:3)? There must also be a repentance of sin along with belief. What about

the conversation we should have regarding Luke 14:28, which says we must "count the cost" as we decide to follow Jesus? That conversation won't happen unless the relationship is real. And finally, as followers of Christ we are to be baptized—by His grace and through our faith we are united with Christ, forgiven of sin, and born again (Matthew 28:18–20; Acts 2:36–38). How can I bring a person to this truth without first establishing a *real* relationship with them? Just as it did in the early church, this call to accept Christ as Lord and Savior will radically change lives and will grow the Lord's body in both numbers and in love.

2. *All Christians are called to be disciples.* Jesus commanded His disciples to "go and make disciples" (Matthew 28:18). That command was not exclusive to just those few men. We know this because they taught others to be disciples, who taught others, and so on. I have an extremely difficult time understanding how many "Christians" in the church today will never speak to anyone outside of church about Jesus. Very few people are intentionally connecting to others within their sphere of influence, be it coworkers, family members, friends, or acquaintances outside of church. Very few are working to develop a relationship that will enable them to evangelize. The truth is that if we are not doing this, we are *willfully* disobeying a command of Christ. As with Point 1, how can we possibly hope to begin a dialogue about this topic (the converted person now reaching out to the lost to convert others) if there is not a *real* relationship?

3. *Unity and community must be in Jesus Christ's church.* As Jesus said, "By this all men will know that you are my disciples, if you love one another" (John 13:35). How do we put this into actual practice in today's church? How do we restore the church to once again becoming a close spiritual family, not just a Sunday morning event? How does the church put into practice God's command to love one another, to encourage each other, to admonish and teach each other, and to confess our sins to one another, for example? When we do these things, the result will be a church that grows closer to each other. A community

with unity, becoming warm and affectionate not only to each other but to visitors as well. A community of believers that no longer gets caught up in pettiness, in power struggles, in egos, and all the divisive things that tend to split congregations. When this happens, one can anticipate and expect exponential growth.

4. *The Holy Spirit must indwell within the church.* This is probably one of the most controversial topics in conservative churches today, and sadly, it is ignored for that very reason. But here is the fact of the matter: this is the power of God at work in his people. Scripture is not hard to understand on this. When we are baptized, we are, by grace, not only forgiven but also given the Holy Spirit (Acts 2:38). Romans 8, Ephesians 1, and many other passages in the New Testament give us beautiful promises that the Holy Spirit gives us not only the assurance of pardon but also power! God does more in our lives and His church by the power of the Spirit than we can ever ask for or imagine (Ephesians 3:20–21)!

Do we abandon our new converts at this time because our relationship is not advanced to the point where we can properly explain this oft-misunderstood concept? I feel very confident in making this accusation against the church today. We have totally dropped the ball in this area and from what I can tell, we don't really want to pick it up. We fear being labeled as a group of ultra-liberal Pentecostal zealots. The fact is we cannot and should not deny the power of the Holy Spirit in our lives, but we have denied it and our silence on the subject convicts us. The result of this Holy Spirit suppression is evident. Disconnected church families struggling to hold onto the pretense of a unified and loving community of believers who share a passion for Jesus and His church.

These four points must once again become part of our belief structure. Every time we identify a person whom we feel led to befriend (in hopes of discipling), we must do so with these four principles firmly established as the goal of why we are developing that specific relationship in the first place. If you are wanting to become friends with a person for any other reason, I'm suggesting that you are on the wrong track and looking to form a relationship, not to save a person from eternal separation from their Creator, but instead for some type of personal reward or gain. It may not be something overtly selfish either. Perhaps you are lonely and you like a person. You are only looking for some companionship, nothing more, nothing less. Is that wrong? But remember, Jesus said we need to be all in. Playing both sides of the fence (one foot in the spiritual world and one foot in the physical world) won't cut it. That lukewarm spirituality is repulsive to Jesus (Revelation 3:15–16). Why become friends with anyone if not for the purpose of saving their soul? Nothing else matters.

10

ESTABLISHING TRUST AND EMOTIONAL INVESTMENT

We are finally getting to the payoff from all the work that has been done so far: from taking inventory, to building various leadership teams, and incorporating intentional activities that have the specific purpose of cultivating meaningful relationships. Once we have established a meaningful relationship with another person, we are now at the point where trust and emotional investments can be made. It is in this particular time and place that we have the freedom to engage our friend with the most important question that can ever be asked of another human: Do you believe that Jesus Christ is the Son of God and that He died on the cross for your sins? Getting to this point involves a lot of emotional expenditure, and it requires a level of trust given to you by the person you are hoping to bring to Christ.

As young adults, emotional safety becomes increasingly important and finding a person with whom we can exercise deeper levels of transparency is a significant developmental milestone. It is usually a trial-and-error activity whereby we use past relationships to inform the degree to which we allow others into our confidence. This is why a person's character and integrity, or lack thereof, is so important. Imagine the damage that is done when a person claiming to be a Christian manipulates another individual, gaining their trust, and then uses personal information that was shared in confidence to control and coerce.

Unfortunately, I have worked with a few students who have experienced these types of relationships. They gave their trust to an individual who lacked integrity. When this person claims to be a Christian, the damage to the church is inconceivable and often changes the entire trajectory of a young person's life who is trying to learn about Christ. If fact, it may very well cause that person to leave their faith before it ever really begins.

Most of what I want to say over these next few pages you know already. In fact, I almost did not include this chapter because I felt it was stating the obvious. However, as I began to think about what trust really means, especially from a spiritual perspective, and how badly we can mess things up when we break trust with another person, I decided to go ahead and state the obvious for several reasons.

First, putting our trust in any person carries an element of risk because humans are flawed, and we make mistakes. David understood this well: "It is better to take refuge in the LORD than to trust in man" (Psalm 118:8). Jeremiah also warned us: "Thus says the LORD: Cursed is the man who trusts in man and makes flesh his strength, whose heart turns away from the LORD" (Jeremiah 17:5). Based on the collective counseling sessions I have had with students over the years and their similar experiences with broken trust, there exists an inherent risk in allowing oneself to become vulnerable. I had one student tell me, "I will never trust another person again as long as I live!" It seems there is a contradiction here. On one hand, I am advocating for us to put ourselves in a position where we have gained a person's trust so we can be more effective in sharing Christ. On the other hand, I am basically saying that we humans are not to be trusted. Stay with me.

Second, the more I thought about it, the more I realized that there is another aspect of trust that needs to be discussed. This trust falls into two categories, one being a dual relationship between parent and child, and one being a triad between parent, child, and ministry. We can understand this relationship within the context of a macro perspective (colleges, groups, ministries), and a micro perspective (parents, ministers, mentors, students).

What is trust? Typically, we understand trust to be a firm belief in the reliability, truth, ability, or strength of someone or something. Therein lies the obvious problem. Looking at each of these descriptors, one can see how quickly things go sideways. Are you a reliable person? If someone were to ask me, I would not hesitate to say, "Yes!" But if I'm being honest, I have let people down in the past. Sometimes there were elements outside of my control, like when my car wouldn't start, and someone was relying on me to pick them up. Are you truthful? We all want to say that we are, but all of us have told lies. Are you a capable individual? I suppose it depends on the situation. I have so many humorous anecdotal stories of students asking me for help on different things where they believed I had the ability or knowledge to help them. My heart was in the right place, and I often truly believed I had the capability to help them, but in the end, I found myself trying to explain why things went badly.

Most of us can relate to similar situations. We want to help, and we often believe we are more capable than what we really are. That is the point that David and Jeremiah made. God has unlimited capacity. He is perfect in every way; therefore, it makes sense to put our trust in the one who is truly worthy of our trust. But this does not mean that we cannot rely on one another.

At this point I would like to use an example that will lead into the issues of trust from a macro perspective. Suppose you needed to have heart surgery due to some blockage in your arteries. Even though a plumber understands blockages, he is not the person you are going to trust in this situation. Your faith will be better placed in the hands of a skilled heart surgeon who has performed this operation. However, if the pipes in your house are blocked, the plumber makes more sense. This is obvious and no one in their right mind would have a plumber do open heart surgery.

My father has had two bypass surgeries in his life. The decision on where to go, which surgeon to use, what type of aftercare was needed, what facilities had the best post-surgery programs, and many other considerations were carefully researched. Why not just pick the first surgeon that popped up on the internet? Or why not just wander into whatever hospital was closest to us and roll the dice? We know the answer, right? A life was on the line. We wanted to make sure he went to the best. Using every resource available to us, we dug into the work, we checked references, we asked lots of questions, and we consulted. In the end, we made an informed decision.

You know what's funny? Even with plumbers, most of us do the same thing, don't we? Make some calls, find the best rates, ask other people if they know of a good plumber. It is not a life on the line, but we still put at least some effort and energy into a decision as trivial as finding a decent plumber. Where am I going with all this?

Trust is a matter of faith in someone or something. What we are talking about here isn't the pipes in your house, or even a life. We are talking about the eternal. The forever. How much work, research, consultation, reference checking, interviewing, and question asking is happening before a decision is made on where you and your adult children will be placing their trust when they leave home for college? You need to understand that college is more serious than the front lines of any war that has ever been fought in human history, except it is spiritual instead of physical, and the outcome of that war determines where your child spends all of eternity!

Listen to this: In the ten years that I have been leading a campus ministry, I have had less than twenty parents come talk to me about their child's spiritual needs, our program, or the churches in the area. Early on in my campus ministry career, I made excuses for parents. Maybe they didn't know that college is where two out of three will walk away from Christianity. Perhaps they didn't know the risks. Maybe they didn't know who to call or contact. Maybe they didn't know that there are resources and ministries at colleges to help keep their children faithful.

Today, I have stopped making excuses for parents. The fact is most parents do not care about the eternity of their children's souls, and I don't say that lightly. I realize this is a brutal accusation to level at any person. In fact, I have deleted and retyped that last sentence numerous times. I finally decided to take a risk and leave it in because I cannot, in all honesty, find another reason. The evidence is damning. What parent, who truly cares about eternal consequences, makes no effort to seek the continued spiritual nurturing of their child when they leave home? That same parent will move heaven and earth to ensure that their child gets into the right fraternities or sororities. They will spend countless hours making sure their child gets the most out of college from an educational and social perspective. Yet when it comes to spiritual needs, they make no visits to the churches located in that city. They make no calls to campus ministries. They do nothing to meet and interview the people who would have endeavored to teach, mentor, and protect the precious soul of their child. Let me say it again. In my ten-plus years of campus ministry, I have had fewer than twenty sets of parents engage me about our ministry and the spiritual journey awaiting their college-aged son or daughter—out of multiple hundreds of students.

Though they are very few, I am so thankful for the parents who get it. Parents that do the work. They understand that their child is walking onto the front lines of a battlefield. They ensure that their child has the best weapons and resources not only to survive the war but also to thrive amid the battle. Those of us who are working on the front lines of the spiritual war have seen you, and we cherish the example you set for the rest. However, if you are one of the many parents who have not done your work, you should be aware of how your spiritual neglect for your children will impact them in this next phase of their life. You have a responsibility that does not end just because your child has left your house for college.

Might this be related to a pattern that we have set within the church? I'm talking about the pattern where parents have been conditioned to hand off the spiritual welfare of their children to the youth minister? Maybe. Regardless of the reason, it is time for us to work together and combine our resources. It is time for you to evaluate me and the other surgeons tending to the spiritual obstructions that your child will face—obstructions that eventually lead to spiritual death. You have a responsibility to your child to know the surgeons, the procedures, the expectations and success rates, and the programs.

Just as you know how important it is to find the best heart surgeon to operate on a loved one, how much more important is the work that can save the soul of your child? Why put your trust in the unknown? Why leave it to chance that your child will eventually stumble into a ministry that has a capable program that will guide, guard, and protect? It is imperative that you do the homework that is needed and allow the choice of colleges to be led by the spiritual programs on campus rather than the social programs.

As a parent, one of the most important decisions you and your college student will make is whom to trust with their continued spiritual development. This is the time to have one of the most transparent and genuine conversations of your life with your child. If you have never demonstrated the importance of spiritual things in your home, it is not too late. Own your mistakes. Tell your teen that you are sorry. Do not make excuses. Tell them how important it is for them to get plugged in to a good campus ministry and to find a church. Do this work together so your actions match your words. Make time for heartfelt conversations regarding the next step in their spiritual journey.

I have had discussions with students who told me that their parents did just this. It was transformational. Rather than accusing their mom or dad of being hypocritical, it initiated a spark that led to a spiritual reawakening for parent and child. This is a great place to start laying the groundwork for trusting a specific person. What better example for a child who is about to leave for college than to have the assurance in knowing their parent's highest concern is for their spiritual welfare?

Likewise, the parents and child both need to embark on the journey of establishing a trusting relationship with the person (or people) who will have a spiritual influence during the child's college years. This should be done together so the child witnesses their parents' vested interest. The same goes with finding a sound church home for the student. How does this look from a practical standpoint?

First, you must visit in person. The more times, the better. I have had those few engaged parents show up at our campus ministry unannounced, and I think that is awesome! Scheduled visits are also appreciated but showing up unexpectedly is also a good practice. If you find a campus minister who has a problem with unannounced visits, let that be a warning sign that something is amiss. Second, talk to other students who have attended that campus ministry or church. If they have student leaders in the ministry, make the time to interview them about the ministry. Talk to the minister at the church where most of the college students attend. Ask questions about how many students regularly attend worship services and classes. Third, talk to the campus minister. Get as much information about the program, weekly events, mission work, student activities, leadership structure, small groups, Bible classes, outreach efforts, campus events, etc. Fourth, do some social media stalking. It is amazing how much can be learned from the social media accounts of a campus ministry. Finally, and I've already said it, but it is worth repeating. Visit as much as you can. That is the only way to get a real vibe of what a ministry is all about, and ministries who care about your kid will *never* have a problem with you showing up whenever. Don't forget that.

Included in the resource section of this book is a list of questions that I have been asked by parents and students over the years. These questions are excellent ways to get a lot of information in a short amount of time. Getting the answers to these questions in person is good, but I would recommend emailing the questions you want answered to the campus minister for two reasons. One, you have the answers in writing, and two, you get to see the responsiveness of the campus minister. I will add to this last comment that campus ministers who are doing their job the right way will be extremely busy. That said, if they don't get back to you within a week, I would advise sending a reminder and a phone call. If another week goes by without reply, consider that as a red flag.

Our goal, as a campus ministry, is to bring students to Christ. This could be your child, whom you thought was already a Christian, but they never developed their own faith. Sometimes this will be a student who knows nothing about the Bible, or possibly a student who has fallen away and is searching for a way back. The point is without someone who has gained the student's trust, the odds are not in their favor of finding Jesus during their college years. Again, the model is simple. Take inventory, build a team, provide activities, develop relationships, and establish trust. There is one final step after trust is gained, but that comes next. It should be emphasized that each of these steps builds upon the next. One cannot have the type of conversations needed to bring a person to Christ without first having a relationship with the person.

As a parent, youth minister, or church leader, it is important to know that college students have grown more cynical over the years. We are living in a world where almost everything we see or hear is fake. And before anyone gets "triggered," I am not getting political. Ask any child who has access to social media, and they will be able to tell you just how fake our society has become. This is so important to understand as we work on developing our relationships with a generation who has grown up in a postmodern world. The concept boils down to genuine versus disingenuous. The latter is the natural default, and this mindset dominates and informs the decision-making processes of most young people. One might begin to see the complexity when a Christian student wants to have a genuine discussion about Christ with a nonbeliever.

I'm sharing this because there was a time when one could initiate a conversation about Jesus with an acquaintance or even a stranger and nothing would seem amiss. In fact, I remember my grandfather doing this while standing in line at a grocery store. Not only were his questions about a person's soul answered, but they were also well received by most. As surprising as it may sound, he was able to get strangers in a grocery store to schedule a Bible study with him! I have tried this tactic numerous times. In grocery stores, pumping gas, at coffee shops, or wherever an opportunity presented itself. Here are a few examples of some responses I have gotten:

- "I'm already a Christian."
- "I'm good."
- "Not for me."
- "I don't believe in God, and I don't need you trying to convince me."
- "Does this usually work for you?"
- "Get away from me."
- "Not interested."
- "Dude! Are you serious right now?"

A few have been overtly hostile, but most are simply annoyed that I am messing up their day with spiritual talk.

As we think about this, I would ask the reader to reflect on what was happening in the first century as the church exploded in number. What parallels can be drawn from what we are doing at our campus ministry and what Jesus was doing while He was establishing His church?

My first observation is a model based upon mobile small groups, a few select individuals whom He developed into apostles. A second observation is that people were coming to Him because He was offering something they wanted. Word had spread about His abilities, and people wanted to see Him heal or be healed themselves. A third observation is that Jesus healed people for the express purpose of teaching them. In other words, He had a captive audience, and He made the most of it. A fourth observation is that He was intentionally relational, which caused people to put their faith in Him. This was a model of discipling that worked then, and it works now.

Some might say, "But Jesus was able to get people together because He was able to perform great miracles." My response is that we do the same thing with our activities. That is the point. Do things that will pull people together. As much as social media is an evil upon this world, as Christians, we can utilize it for good by advertising events and activities that can be enjoyed.

In the end, all these steps must lead us to a place where people will let their guard down. We must get them to a place where they will be less cynical and know that we are genuine in our message. They may not agree with it right away, or they may not understand it, but what they will know is that we are being honest. We have developed a relationship with them, and they know our intentions are pure, and *that* is why trust is so important.

11

CONVERTING TRUST INTO SPIRITUAL COMMITMENT

I have made several attempts writing this chapter because of the inherent subjectiveness in trying to identify the point at which trust is converted into a spiritual commitment. Going back through ten years of notes and interviews with students has offered me some insight, but in truth, only the individual knows in their heart whether they have fully given themselves to Christ. Another potential issue is that by using some objective standard to identify the point at which an individual makes a spiritual commitment to Christ requires me to use a personal doctrinal belief with which some may take issue. After weeks of study, prayer, and re-writing, I settled on using this doctrinal position because it highlights several flaws within postmodern denominationalism that I must deal with every year. So as you read through this chapter, I ask you to keep an open mind. Rather than discarding my words because you may not agree with my position, look past the points of contention, and recognize the bigger issues that I will point out. With that said, I will be discussing several components of salvation that include hearing God's Word, belief/faith, repentance, confession, baptism, and grace. First, I would like to share multiple conversion stories recorded in the Bible so you can see what my students see as they read (some for the first time) stories that were never shared with them.

In Acts 2, Luke recorded the events leading up to Peter's sermon on the day of Pentecost, which must have been an amazing event to witness as the Holy Spirit was poured out upon the apostles. Shortly after, Peter talked to all the people gathered there in Jerusalem, proclaiming Jesus as both Lord and the Christ, reminding them that Jesus was the one whom they had just crucified. Luke said:

> Now when they *heard* this they were cut to the heart, and said to Peter and the rest of the apostles, "Brothers, what shall we do?" And Peter said to them, "*Repent* and be *baptized* every one of you in the name of Jesus Christ *for the forgiveness of your sins* and you will receive the gift of the Holy Spirt." (Acts 2:37–38)

In Acts 8 we are told about Philip and the Ethiopian eunuch, who was a court official of Candace, queen of the Ethiopians. This court official was in a chariot traveling back home from Jerusalem, where he had been worshiping, and he was studying the book of Isaiah in the Old Testament. Philip asked the court official if he understood what he was reading, to which the eunuch replied, "How can I, *unless someone guides me?*" At this point, the eunuch invited Philip to sit with him, and Philip shared the good news of Jesus. Then Luke wrote:

> And as they were going along the road they came to some water, and the eunuch said, "See, here is water! What prevents me from being *baptized?*" And he commanded the chariot to stop, and they both went down into the water, Philip and the eunuch, and he *baptized* him. (Acts 8:36–38)

As we move through the book of Acts, we are introduced to Saul who was persecuting Christians. Saul was on his way to the city of Damascus to seek out other Christians and bring them back to Jerusalem to be persecuted. On his way, he was struck blind by Jesus. As Saul fell to the ground, blinded, we read:

"Saul, Saul, why are you persecuting me?" And he said, "Who are you, Lord?" And he said, "I am Jesus, whom you are persecuting. But rise and enter the city, and you will be told what you are to do." (Acts 9:4–5)

So Saul went on to Damascus where he met a man named Ananias, whom Jesus had instructed to lay hands on Saul to heal him:

So Ananias departed and entered the house. And laying hands on him he said, "Brother Saul, the Lord Jesus who appeared to you on the road by which you came has sent me so that you may regain your sight and be filled with the Holy Spirit." And immediately something like scales fell from his eyes, and he regained his sight. Then he rose and *was baptized*; and taking food he was strengthened. (Acts 9:17–19)

In Acts 10 we are told that Peter traveled to Caesarea to convert a man named Cornelius. Peter went to the home of Cornelius and told him and his family about Jesus and how He was put to death and was raised by God on the third day. Peter told them that everyone who believes in Jesus receives forgiveness of sins through His name:

"Can anyone withhold water for baptizing these people, who have received the Holy Spirit just as we have?" And he *commanded them to be baptized in the name of Jesus Christ.* (Acts 10:47–48)

In Acts 13, Luke turned his narrative back to Saul and the missionary journey that Saul and Barnabas began together. Coming to Philippi, Saul, who was now going by the name of Paul, went outside the city gates down to the riverside to pray. Gathered there was a group of women. Paul preached to them about Jesus:

One who *heard* us was a woman named Lydia, from the city of Thyatira, a seller of purple goods, who was a worshiper of God.

The Lord opened her heart to pay attention to what was said by Paul. And after *she was baptized*, and her household as well, she urged us, saying, "If you have judged me to be faithful to the Lord, come to my house and stay." And she prevailed upon us. (Acts 16:14–15)

After the conversion of Lydia, we read that Paul and Silas are put into prison. Luke tells us that around midnight Paul and Silas were praying and singing hymns when there was an earthquake that opened all the doors to the prison. When the jailer awakened and saw all the doors open, he was about to kill himself, but Paul cried out for him to stop, telling him that no one had left. This presented an opportunity for Paul to teach the jailer about Jesus:

Then he brought them out and said, "Sirs, *what must I do to be saved?*" And they said, "*Believe* in the Lord Jesus, and you will be saved, you and your household." And they spoke the word of the Lord to him and to all who were in his house. And he took them the same hour of the night and washed their wounds; and *he was baptized at once*, he and all his family. (Acts 16:30–33)

In Acts 17:30:

The times of ignorance God overlooked, but now he commands all people everywhere to *repent*, because he has fixed a day on which he will judge the world in righteousness by a man whom he has appointed; and of this he has given assurance to all by raising him from the dead.

In Acts 18:8:

Crispus, the ruler of the synagogue, *believed* in the Lord, together with his entire household. And many of the Corinthians hearing Paul *believed* and *were baptized*.

In Peter's first letter to the exiles of the Dispersion in Pontus, Galatia, Cappadocia, Asia, and Bithynia, he wrote:

> For Christ also suffered once for sins, the righteous for the unrighteous, that he might bring us to God, being put to death in the flesh but made alive by the spirit, in which he went and proclaimed to the spirits in prison, because they formerly did not obey, when God's patience waited in the days of Noah, while the ark was being prepared, in which a few, that is, eight persons, were brought safely through water. *Baptism, which corresponds to this, now save you*, not as a removal of direct from the body but as an appeal to God for a good conscience, through the resurrection of Jesus Christ, who has gone into heaven and is at the right hand of God, with angels, authorities, and powers having been subjected to him. (1 Peter 3:18–22)

In his letter to the church in Rome, Paul wrote:

> How can we who died to sin still live in it? Do you not know that all of us who have been *baptized into Christ Jesus were baptized into his death*? We were buried therefore with him by baptism into death, in order that, just as Christ was raised from the dead by the glory of the Father, we too might walk in newness of life. (Romans 6:2–4)

With the above verse in mind, written by Paul, I want to go back to Acts 22 to get a little more context about Saul's conversion. These are the words of Ananias, as recorded by Luke, concerning Paul's conversion:

> And he said, "The God of our fathers appointed you to know his will, to see the Righteous One and to hear a voice from his mouth; for you will be a witness for him to everyone of what you have seen and hear. And now *why do you wait? Rise*

and be baptized and wash away your sins, calling on his name." (Acts 22:14–16)

All these verses demonstrate the context that surrounded a non-believer's conversion into Christ. They were firsthand accounts written by the apostles or those who knew them. But what about Jesus? What did He have to say about converting trust into a spiritual commitment? Read the following passages:

And Jesus came and said to them, "All authority in heaven and on earth has been given to me. Go therefore and make disciples of all nations, *baptizing them in the name of the Father and of the Son and of the Holy Spirit*, teaching them to observe all that I have commanded you. And behold I am with you always, to the end of the age." (Matthew 28:18–20)

And he said to them, "Go into all the world and proclaim the gospel to the whole creation. Whoever *believes and is baptized will be saved*, but whoever does not believe will be condemned." (Mark 16:15–16)

Now there was a man of the Pharisees name Nicodemus, a ruler of the Jews. This man came to Jesus by night and said to him, "Rabbi, we know that you are a teacher come from God, for no one can do these signs that you do unless God is with him." Jesus answered him, "Truly, truly, I say to you, *unless one is born again, he cannot see the kingdom of God.*" Nicodemus said to him, "How can a man be born when he is old? Can he enter a second time into his mother's womb and be born?" Jesus answered, "Truly, truly, I say to you, *unless one is born of water and the Spirit*, he cannot enter the kingdom of God. That which is born of the flesh is flesh, and that which is born of the Spirit is spirit." (John 3:1–6)

Through the examples set forth in the New Testament, we begin to see a very clear picture emerge of how trust is converted into a spiritual commitment that carries extraordinary implications to our salvation. In case you missed the key elements that are repeated, they include the teaching and hearing of the good news (that is the gospel) of Jesus dying on the cross for our sin and being raised by God on the third day. It includes coming to believe that Jesus is God's Son and making a confession of faith. It includes repenting of one's sins and then being baptized in the name of Jesus Christ for the forgiveness of sins. These are not suggestions. These are commandments given by Jesus. Some people teach that baptism is not one of the things that needs to happen to have forgiveness of sins. However, as you have read through these verses, coming to that conclusion is contradictory to what Jesus and the apostles taught.

Being committed to Christ requires obedience to his commands. We can't pick and choose which ones we want to follow and which ones we discount or minimize. Some people teach that to enter God's kingdom, all we need to do is have faith in Jesus. Some teach that God's grace is the only thing needed. Some teach that confessing Jesus is all that is needed, and still others teach that if one is baptized, that is sufficient. The truth, according to the Bible, is that all these elements are necessary. There is a reason behind each one, and it is not our job (nor do we have the authority) to decide which one takes precedent or which one is not a requisite for salvation.

Here is my point: unless we teach the whole truth, we cannot convert trust into a spiritual commitment. In fact, we surrender our credibility when we begin teaching man-made edicts that stray from our biblical examples. Time and again I find myself across from students who have never been shown the verses that began this chapter. I must wonder why so many of our young adults have not been encouraged to read the New Testament books that teach the principles of our salvation in their entirety. This partial truth teaching is the very thing that creates an environment of mistrust. In a society where the prevalent attitude among our young is one of cynicism, why are so many religious leaders pushing agendas filled with half-truths?

Over the last decade I have been fortunate enough to have hundreds of conversations with students about who taught them, how they were taught, and what they thought about the many doctrinal beliefs that differ from one denomination to another. It is remarkable how many students share the same story. They grew up in a church that taught one specific doctrine, but there was never any encouragement to study for themselves. Some asked their church leaders some difficult questions and were simply told that their way was the right way and that their interpretation of Scripture was built upon countless generations. At some point, these traditional belief systems became so inculcated, that any questions regarding obvious conflicts with Scripture had stopped being asked centuries ago.

Today, we have a vast network of well-meaning Christians teaching a modified version of the gospel because that is what they were taught. Unfortunately, when I have college students read and study the Gospels, most for the first time in their lives, they become concerned (rightly so) by the contradictions. Not contradictions within Scripture, but contradictions between what they have been taught and what they are reading.

Allow me a moment to pause and admit to you that it would be wrong of me to portray my own doctrinal belief system as completely untethered from bias. Like any person who has been raised within a given culture, ethnicity, socio-economical class, religious affiliation, and a plethora of other influences, we develop a worldview that shapes how we see and interpret everything, including the Bible. Please believe me when I say that I am keenly aware of bias.

I have stopped telling my students what specific denomination I was raised in. To be fully transparent to the reader, I was technically raised within churches of Christ. At least that was the name on the sign outside of the building later in my life. I say technically because my parents were missionaries in Africa for the first part of my life, so church and worship looked very different to me than what we see in most churches today on a given Sunday morning. Our worship was in our home. It was simple yet powerful. We taught the gospel just as it was taught in the first century, just as we read in Acts.

I will also say this. I do not believe any one denomination, including churches of Christ, are 100 percent accurate on every single doctrinal issue that continues to divide the Lord's church. With that said, I want to share something amazing with you.

As I said, when asked by the college students about my own church affiliation, I tell them I do not belong to any one denomination. Just a Christian. And when it concerns the things we do to become a Christian (transitioning our trust into a true spiritual commitment), I only allow God's Word to inform what that looks like. And here is the amazing thing. No matter the denominational background, when I tell my students to "just read" Acts and any of the Gospels, they almost always reach the same conclusions I have reached.

It really is not complicated, but we have allowed centuries of manmade traditions to inform us rather than God's Word. I am not okay with how much the church has changed over the centuries, including my own faith background. I am not okay with how disconnected we have become. I pass a church on my way to work each day whose marquee/billboard advertises three different worship styles. They have a traditional worship, a contemporary worship, and a rock worship, all within the same congregation. They have literally divided their own church into multiple factions just so they can accommodate every different preference.

We do not need a biblical scholar schooled in theology to interpret for us how people were coming to Christ in the first century. We do not need a denominational preacher clarifying how God commands us to be born again, or how we are to be "in Christ." None of these examples and commands in the Bible are confusing, but thanks to denominational teachings, we have polluted and complicated that which was simple and straightforward. And all this leads to mistrust. Mistrust leads to further cynicism. Cynicism leads to doubt. Doubt leads to apathy, and apathy leads to unbelief.

I have found that one of the best ways to maintain a trust that leads to spiritual commitment is to always say to my students, "Please do not take my word for truth. I am human and I am flawed. I want you to study this for yourselves and make sure that what I am teaching not only lines up factually with what Jesus and His apostles taught but is also contextually correct." So we come back to a few specific doctrinal issues that give us some indication that an individual has made a life-changing decision to give their life to Christ.

From my viewpoint, there are very few students, who after reading the Gospels or the book of Acts, are confused about what needs to happen. Like Philip and the Ethiopian eunuch, they understand that baptism was never presented as optional in the Bible. Confessing Christ as Lord was never an option that didn't matter. Repenting of sins was clearly part of the process. Believing that Jesus was God's Son matters. At times, just to make sure we are on the same page, I have used some of the arguments I have heard over the years that discount one or more of these commands.

I will say to the students something like: "You do realize the Bible says that by grace you have been saved through faith. You can read that in Ephesians 2:8–9. So why do you think it is necessary to do all this other stuff?"

The students, having now read Acts or Romans or Matthew, see the incorrect assumption. They respond along these lines: "Yes, that is right! Grace and faith do save! But the Bible also teaches us that there is more to it than that." They will then show me a scripture that talks about repentance and confession and baptism. Even more astute, they point out that just because Ephesians 2 doesn't mention baptism or confession or repentance, other scriptures do not mention grace or faith. Just because one verse does not include grace does not mean that grace is not needed for salvation. And just because a verse only talks about grace or faith does not mean that baptism, confession, and repentance are not necessary. That's why we must read it all.

I must ask: How is it that these young college adults, some of which have never opened a Bible, can understand the simplicity of God's Word better than ministers, priests, and scholars who have studied the Bible their entire lives? The answer is simple. They have shed their bias.

If you are a teacher of God's Word, you hold a great responsibility to teach the truth. God's truth, not man-made edicts and politically correct versions of the gospel. It requires us to reexamine the Scriptures and work diligently to put aside our own worldviews and biases. Accepting the commandments of Jesus forces us to confront centuries of traditional teachings about salvation, worship, the Lord's Supper, and the Holy Spirit, just to name a few.

How does one reconcile generations of family members who were God-fearing people—good people—but were taught baptism or some other clear command connected to salvation was optional? Clearly, Jesus taught something completely different about baptism, as did his apostles. What about godly family members who were baptized but had no desire or inclination to tell others about Jesus and died without ever sharing the good news with another person? Are we to feel confident that those beloved family members are in heaven? How does one reconcile generations of people who died without confessing Jesus as the Son of God or failing to recognize the saving power of grace?

Do we, like so many others down through the centuries have done, create plausible-sounding doctrine that somehow exonerates a person's disobedience because the truth is something we cannot understand or handle? That is exactly what has happened, and hundreds of years later, these distorted versions of the gospel and the plan for our salvation have been accepted as truth, as scripture, firmly concreted into centuries-old doctrine. Here we are today with generations of young adults who have never read what the Bible actually teaches. Just like us, they have accepted certain teaching as fact, be it from their parents, priests, friends, and ministers.

This is the context of most students when they arrive at our ministry, and year after year I watch them battle through the concerns and questions that will naturally arise when they read the Bible for themselves and begin to see the gaps. They discover that what they have been taught is only partially true. Often, these students enter a theological struggle within themselves. Do they believe what they have been taught so they do not have to consider the implications of loved ones who died outside of Christ? Or do they accept what the Bible teaches as authoritative and begin the painful work of coming to terms with the potential that loved ones may have entered eternity in a state of uncertainty?

This may be why "speak your truth" has become such a powerful declaration amongst high school and college students. In essence, whatever makes them comfortable becomes their truth. It is a way to expel from one's life any kind of objective moral that might cause discomfort, and I will be the first to admit that there are many passages of Scripture that cause me no small discomfort.

God is not the author of confusion. Not all, but most are able to accept the fact that salvation is not a one-principal proposition. Instead, salvation requires obedience on several key items. Our students talk at length about mercy and grace. They talk about love and about how God does not wish any to perish, but the path that leads to destruction is broad and the gate is wide, and many will walk this path. They talk about how the path that leads to life is narrow, and the gate is small, and only a few find it. It is at this point that many students begin to understand that the theology they were taught allows for many to find the narrow path, which contradicts what Jesus was teaching in Matthew 7.

Truth or lies. Trust or mistrust. It is tempting to water down different parts of apostolic commands and examples. It is also tempting to skim over what Jesus taught because some of His teachings are hard. But in the end, we have done far more damage by teaching half-truths, assuming that the pill was too bitter to swallow, rather than acknowledging the facts. Some of our loved ones did pass away never knowing the full truth or believing something contrary to Scripture. What does that mean for their eternity? Honestly, none of us know for sure. Again, we hope and pray that God has some provision, and that grace is even more than what we could ever hope.

However, I do not think it does any good to present anything different than what the Bible teaches us. Salvation is conditional. Many who claim to be Christians, who appear to be Christians, who do great works in the name of Christ, will not be in heaven (Matthew 7:22). My hope is that one day every denomination will toss out all man-made doctrines and return to the teaching of the New Testament. Nothing more, nothing less. Only by doing this will the Lord's church enter an age where trust is placed entirely on Jesus Christ and not on man.

I know this chapter might have been controversial to some, but I believe that it is possible to objectively discern when and how one's trust in a person who is teaching the truth of the gospel in its fullness converts that trust into a spiritual commitment to Christ. The emptying of self and being filled with Christ is a transcendent moment. Like those who stood before Peter as he told them they had crucified the Son of God, we also stand guilty before His throne. And like them, we should cry out, "What must we do?" Peter's response has not changed, and the truth of our salvation remains the same just as it did for those who heard his words on that day of Pentecost: "Repent and be baptized every one of you in the name of Jesus Christ for the forgiveness of your sins." I cannot think of a better objective point at which a person fully gives themselves over to Christ than through the immersion in the watery grave, rising again, just as Christ rose from the dead, a new creature in Christ.

12

CREATING SMALL GROUPS

I n the previous chapter it was necessary to cover some of the objective indicators that allow us to have a reference point regarding one's conversion into a spiritually committed relationship with Christ. The reason is because we used those reference points (specifically baptism) as leading indicators. This may not sound significant or particularly relevant to our discussion. At least not until a global pandemic enters the world.

Halfway through 2020 I began to develop an autonomous reactionary response anytime I heard the word COVID, along with many other people. According to a *Forbes* report, using only one social media platform, the word was mentioned by over 6.7 million people in a single day. This does not include other social media platforms, newspapers, television, magazines, articles, speeches, or the simple day-to-day conversations between people.[15] I am sharing this because I want you to know that there is a significant development related to COVID and how we view discipling within the church that I believe every person should know. Otherwise, I would never mention the word again. But before I share what I now know, without a doubt, to be the lifeblood of any church or ministry, allow me to set the foundation.

Bishop Mark Dyer said, "About every five hundred years the empowered structures of institutionalized Christianity, whatever they may be at that time, become an intolerable carapace that must be shattered in order that renewal and growth may occur."[16] From a historical (and factual) perspective, we see this to be true. Recall Gregory the Great during the sixth century ushering in the period that we call the Dark Ages. Then in 1054, a second span of five hundred years begins the Great Schism that ensured the wedging of Eastern Orthodoxy and Western Roman Catholicism. Moving forward another five hundred years, another upheaval occurs when Martin Luther produced his ninety-five theses in Wittenberg in 1517. Moving forward another five years brings us to 2017.

The church is positioned for another major upheaval, and I believe the doors that were being slowly opened that would usher in a new era just got blown apart by COVID. What we are looking at right now is not so much a reformation due to a corrupt and apostate church as was the case during Luther's time, but rather, a reformation in response to an irrelevant church in relation to its primary function and task.[17] COVID exposed the complete brokenness of what it is that we (the church) are supposed to be doing, namely relational discipling.

"COVID-19 also calls us to reimagine the idea of church as community. The call to community is central to the Christian faith and practice. The very notion of community is established in the Godhead; God is community (Trinity), and the church (*ekklesia*) refers to a community whether it is a local church, a citywide church or as the universal church."[18] During the last five years Christianity has continued to move further away from family as organized religion began to dominate the spiritual landscape, which resulted in more and more artificial performances in large, ornate buildings that look nothing like real life.

Author Wolfgang Simson wrote in *Houses That Change the World: The Return of House Churches* that we have moved further away from a relational way of doing church. For example, instead of moving from house to house, we meet inside large buildings. Instead of sharing all we have, we tithe. Our lifestyle is individualistic instead of community based. We work to get people into a church building rather than inside a home. Rather than making disciples, our philosophy is to make members.[19] COVID has forced us back to our roots (at least temporarily) as churches were closed. Many have opened back up as of the time of this writing, but many closed for good. Across the world, the church was forced to move back home, literally, which is where it all began—in homes and small groups. Consider this quote by Niemandt from his speech in Cape Town, South Africa, in 2016:

> The church needs to establish a faithful presence in the commons. Faithful presence means, taking your bodies, your location, and your community very seriously, as seriously as God in Christ took them: Faithful presence invites you to act on the belief that God is giving you what you need to be formed as disciples within your location. Faithful presence implies a specific kind of presence in all the places that Christians find themselves—and in such a way that it affirms the integrity of Christian faith.[20]

I hope you will reflect on this historical context considering what I am about to share with you because it is too important to discount, especially if you are serious about the fight our children are in, the state of our churches, and even your own spiritual practices. For our college ministry, nothing really changed. We were bringing souls to Christ before the pandemic, and the number of conversions during the height of the pandemic basically stayed the same. While churches were losing members and closing, our student center was thriving. Why? How in the world was this even possible? I was asked that question many times. The answer was simple: small groups. So let's talk about this for a moment and hopefully you will leave this chapter excited and ready to walk through the doors that COVID blew apart.

Clearly, the concept of small groups is nothing new. They have been part of churches for decades, with varied success. They peaked during the late 1970s and 1980s. Within conservative churches, small groups began to fall out of favor due to some bad players, as I mentioned in the chapter on developing relationships. Because of this, many churches discontinued small groups or shut them down before they had time to develop. This was a huge mistake, and I believe the absence of small groups within churches is the primary reason why church membership has trended downward over the last several decades.

Think about how many people have been converted to Christ by inviting them to large worship settings. If you can get them to come at all, this can be an intimidating and overwhelming environment for someone who has never been in a church. If you are lucky enough to be part of a church with robust small groups, it is much easier to invite someone into this environment, and the likelihood that a meaningful Bible study emerges with that person is much greater.

At our ministry, small groups are the lifeblood of our outreach and discipling. Almost every one-on-one Bible study that takes place happens because of small groups. Within the setting of a small group, real relationships are formed. That is hard to accomplish in a church setting where there are hundreds of people. Small groups allow for deeper, intimate relationships to develop, and it is in this setting that trust is established.

However, the risks are still there. Getting great small group leaders who understand the primary objectives and who can effectively guide the group to accomplish those objectives is hard. This is why I included a chapter that talked about leadership development. It is part of the entire process. Randomly throwing a person into this leadership position is a mistake and the likelihood of having an inappropriate (coercive accountability) situation arise is more likely. Again, do not be so afraid of this that you decide the risk outweighs the benefit—because it doesn't if intention and discernment are used when building your leaders and small groups.

Is it necessary to point out that churches have moved away from the biblical model of discipleship? I understand that this may cause some discomfort with some who appreciate the more traditional and conservative approach to church, however, we should not discount the biblical model simply because it causes us discomfort.

I believe there are a few other reasons why we have gotten away from small groups in the home. One reason is because church leaders feel like there is a loss of control. They are not able, in some cases, to experience what is being said and taught, so they fear something incorrect will be taught or something inappropriate might happen. While this is certainly a potential, there are solutions.

Divide the small groups up so that church leadership is represented within each group. That does not mean that the church leaders must oversee the small group, but they can certainly be a participant. A second solution is to begin some ministries that teach and train those who would lead. Again, if we are working toward fellowships that promote trust, leaders should "lead the way."

Another reason why we have moved away from small groups is because people are disconnected from one another. Fewer and fewer families relish the idea of having other church members and strangers in their homes. I do not want to sound overly critical, but if you are one of these people, I encourage you to examine your heart because you are in a very precarious place. How is it that the world will know that we are the disciples of Jesus? By our love. How do we show love? Well, it is certainly not by closing our doors to one another. If you can't agree on this point and see the deep and desperate need to open our homes to small groups, then you are out of sync with who Jesus has called you to be.

A final reason that I will mention (but there are more) is the time commitment. As I have stated earlier, we all have busy lives with many demands and obligations. Finding time to host or be a part of a small group is a big commitment. Just know that once you are part of a healthy and thriving small group, nothing else will be as important. Your small group time will be the thing you will look forward to more than anything else during your week. In fact, you will try to find ways to have small groups as often as possible. Small groups will challenge you and fill you in spiritual ways that you have not begun to imagine.

You will draw closer to God in ways that you never thought possible. But more than any of these things, you will be bringing the lost to Jesus.

I have included several personal stories within this book as a way of illustrating the points I am making. I want to briefly share another with you to demonstrate the power of relational living, small groups, and faith building. One of my former student leaders and his wife (also a former student leader at the CSC) happened to purchase a house next door to my own. That's a story in itself. As college graduates who came through our ministry where small groups were commonplace, this couple started their own small group every Friday night. This is what we all need to be doing because the future of the Lord's church depends on it.

I want to challenge you for a moment. In the last six months, how many people have you had a Bible study with and from that study they gave their life to Christ because of your interaction with them? None? What about the last year? The last five years? I will tell you something shocking. Most regular church attenders who are devout and strong in their faith have not hosted a Bible study, nor have they brought another person to Christ in the last year. If you are one of these people, you need to get angry. You need to start asking yourself why you are not obeying the very last words Jesus spoke to us while on this earth: "Go and make disciples of all nations, baptizing them in the name of the Father and of the Son and of the Holy Spirit" (Matthew 28:19). I cannot imagine standing before the throne of God and having Him say, "Craig, you know what my Son did for you. How many people did you tell?" Then having to answer Him, "None. I told no one what your Son did for me."

We need to stop making excuses. COVID should be an eye-opener for us as well as a primer to begin looking at the model by which we bring the lost to Jesus. I am a living testament to how a relatively ineffective speaker and leader can continue to have success in sharing the good news of Jesus. This has nothing to do with being on campus, having access to students, or having a building to eat in, but it has everything to do with building, sustaining, and pouring into our small groups.

I'm probably like you and not too comfortable inviting someone I don't really know to church. But inviting them over for supper and developing a relationship with them—that's something any of us can do. If I can do it, so can you, so can your youth ministries, and so can most of your church members.

PART 3

THE ROAD

13

BEGINNING THE JOURNEY

Direction, not good intentions, determines your destination. Intuitively, we all know this to be true. I might have the very best intentions to get to Disney World, but if I am not pointed in the right direction, I will not get there no matter how hard I try. Everything I have shared thus far in this book has this principle as a prerequisite. But how do I know if I'm pointed in the right direction? First, I must care. I ask this question of myself quite often when it comes to my job as a campus minister because I have the responsibility to guide your children in a way that is honorable and pleasing to God. This responsibility is something I care about deeply. The consequences of doing my job poorly can have eternal ramifications for your children and for myself.

When I was in the business world, I would occasionally have a manager who reported to me who did not care about their job. Some of them had incredible potential to be fantastic leaders, but they lacked the desire and the initiative to be conscientious about their work. As a result, everything they touched, either directly or indirectly, became infected with their attitude. It always amazed me how one individual could completely change the dynamic of an entire operation with hundreds of employees. If a person does not care enough to continually ask themselves if they are pointed in the right direction, the inevitable result is to miss the intended target. Applying this to our faith walk, one can see how this might take us down some dangerous roads. The person who has stopped caring is truly in a perilous situation.

What I have found to be true more often than not is people do care, but they have gotten sidetracked. They have become disoriented or even lost. Somewhere along the way, something on the side of the road caught their attention, or they stopped following the map. I recall a time when I was consulting with a management group to help them through some environmental concerns. Their facility was located somewhere in the Ozarks, and on my way back home my GPS malfunctioned. I was low on gas, and before too long the sun began to set. It is alarming how swiftly a situation can go from good to bad! I became completely disoriented and hopelessly lost. The sun was setting, I was almost out of gas, and somehow, I had gotten onto a very old gravelly road in the mountains. It was completely dark in the woods, and as I was looking for a place to turn around, I saw an old wooden sign on a crooked post that read . . . and I kid you not: "Dead Woods Cemetery."

Our spiritual journey is fraught with perils. Make no mistake: many of those perils are deliberately placed there by the enemy for the sole purpose of distracting us and causing us to exit the road. When we move away from the Bible, we have, in essence, turned off the GPS that is guiding us back home. Before we even realize what has happened, we find ourselves lost and alone, on a dark road, running out of gas. So always keep your road map by your side, and if what you are doing does not match what the Bible says, then you have departed the road and you are no longer pointed in the right direction. Here is the bad news: Satan has camouflaged the roads that take us in another direction. To us, they look inviting, exciting—not frightening. If only we could see what was really behind all the enticement, it would look more like my journey into Dead Woods Cemetery.

Did you know that most of your kids are arriving at college without a working knowledge of their road map? They have their GPS (Bible) in their hand, but they have no idea how it works or even how to turn it on. If you are part of a group of Christians and just one influential person in your child's life (such as a church leader, pastor, or youth minister) does not really care, the odds are much greater that they have infected more than just your child. A sign that there is disease within your church is a level of apathy and the resistance to change.

Resistance to change is not uncommon, especially in conservative churches who have long-standing traditions. This resistance does not necessarily mean the church has grown apathetic. I want that to be clear. Change for change's sake is not needed. In fact, I find that this rapid kind of transformation is usually in step with church leaders whose desire is to appease the activists pushing for the demise of what they consider to be antiquated and out of touch spirituality and to replace it with a postmodern set of values. However, in some cases people resist necessary and beneficial change that is crucial for church survival.

In Dreher's *The Benedict Option*, he opines about the necessity for radical and broad change within the church at large, much of which revolves around a return to traditional liturgy, and surprisingly, a strong emphasis on smaller home churches. If nothing else, I hope my book has highlighted why change is necessary within our churches considering the causalities to our youth. Perhaps not to the extent that Dreher calls for, but at least in the scope and measure of the biblical model.

We must accept the fact that postmodernism has caused us to drift away from the approach that Jesus used and the way in which nonbelievers were added to the church during the first century. The deniers of this approach are wrong. I have provided a brief glimpse of a model I use, which is closer to the model that Jesus used. I have seen this model work, and I believe churches who are passionate about discipling the lost should be intentional about moving back to this biblical example.

One of the biggest hurdles you will face, assuming that you or your leadership group is allowed to develop a similar approach, will be the inevitable failures. Those who have a hard time with any change will be the first to cry out, "See! I told you this wouldn't work! We need to go back to the way we've always done it!" The reality of the situation is that you will have many starts and stops. Some things will work well, while others will not. People will let you down. Some pivotal, key players will walk away at the very worst time. You will be on the verge of success and that is the moment everything will seem to fall apart. I want to assure you that this process is not easy. It is a completely different prototype, and whoever champions it will need to have remarkable tenacity, thick skin, perseverance, patience, and the ability to control their temper. As I have told others who have worked to return to first-century discipleship, "It is a marathon, not a sprint."

Those who endeavor to turn the tide and change the impact the world is having on our youth need to enter this with the expectation that there will be setbacks and failure. The team needs to understand this too. Being prepared, having a tangible plan with clear objectives and milestones is important. This includes how to respond to those who wish to kill the plan because they are afraid of change, afraid that it is somehow unbiblical or false teaching. These individuals need to be handled with love and care. If they can be shown, through good biblical study, why this approach brings us closer to the Jesus pattern rather than further away, a valuable advocate will be gained who may become one of the program's strongest supporters.

14

GROWING WEARY

For most people, starting a new journey is always exciting. There is so much energy and anticipation. Support is high, and spirits are even higher. Many of us can recall a time in our childhood when we all loaded up in the car or van and began a family vacation. I was always eager to start the journey, but after hours in the car, smashed up against my two siblings in a small hatchback, the trip was not so fun anymore. Arguments began. "Get off me!" "Scoot over!" "EWWW! What's that smell!" Then dad's patience began to wear thin. "So help me, if I have to pull this car over you will all wish we were back home!" The truth of the matter was that it was usually at this point in the trip that I did wish I was back home. I had grown weary, and the excitement was completely gone.

This is life, especially for those who are passionate about being a positive change agent. Weariness creeps in, no matter how hard one might guard against it. For those who love Christ and kingdom work, we are encouraged to remain steadfast. The apostle Paul knew this firsthand.

- "And let us not grow weary of doing good, for in due season we will reap, if we do not give up" (Galatians 6:9).
- "For God is not unjust so as to overlook your work and the love that you have shown for his name in serving the saints, as you still do. And we desire each one of you to show the same earnestness

to have the full assurance of hope until the end, so that you may not be sluggish, but imitators of those who through faith and patience inherit the promises" (Hebrews 6:10–12).

I consider myself fortunate to have stepped into a campus ministry that already had a strong foundation and was firmly established, being the oldest ministry on the university's campus. That said, because it was so firmly established, so too were many traditional expectations that utilized the same "cookie-cutter" recipe that produced the same returns. Nothing seemed out of place or alarming because that model was so ingrained. Previous campus ministers had tried to make some changes, but resistance to any change is part of human nature, and I encountered similar challenges. Plus, I made the mistake of making too many changes all at once. I ran into a brick wall, and I had not even left my driveway. I see resistance to change as one of the biggest reasons why so many good church leaders grow weary prematurely and give up. We can talk about all the effective ways to battle weariness, and there are plenty of great options. However, I have nothing that is more impactful or more powerful than deep and steadfast prayer.

I have not spoken very much about prayer in this book, so I don't want you to get the wrong idea. In fact, the title of this book could easily have been *The Transformational Power of Prayer*. I was eager to do the work, and I could envision a thriving ministry that continually demonstrated the power of God. Further, I had seen God move in mysterious and wonderful ways to bring me into this work. I was as unlikely a candidate for campus ministry as there ever was. I didn't know what God was up to, but I was anxious to see how He was going to use a person such as myself to accomplish His will. Despite all this, I became weary incredibly soon. When I say soon, I mean two days into the job. Literally, my second day. I look back at a situation now and can laugh about it, but in the moment, I was having serious doubts. Allow me to share with you my second day on the job as a campus minister.

I walked into my office and noticed a leak in one of the ceiling tiles. I removed the tile and found a four-inch cast iron pipe had rusted completely through at a coupling joint. I did not have the right tools to fix it myself, so I called a plumber, who arrived that same day. Long story short, the plumber had to remove a six-foot section of pipe and while doing so, it slipped out of his hands and hit him on the head as it fell to the floor. The pipe made a quick pit stop on my desk before crashing on the carpet. This pipe was original to the building, which was built somewhere in the 1890s, and that pipe was the main sewage line for the upstairs apartment. And . . . it was full.

The previous day I had just finished putting all my books, Bibles, and commentaries on the shelves. I am not exaggerating when I say a person could not have covered my office in poop more effectively had they come in with a hose connected to a septic dump truck and sprayed my office from end to end. Somehow that six-foot section of pipe flung fecal matter on my books, the walls, my desk, keyboard, computer, chair, and all over the carpet. (Weeks later, I discovered a brownish material coming out from between the keys on my keyboard when I typed. Obviously, I threw away the keyboard.)

I remember going home that night, only two days on the job, thinking I had made an incredibly foolish decision. The doubts started to creep in at that point. *Why did I leave a good job with benefits? What qualifies me to be a minister? Who will take me seriously?* I didn't have any degrees in theology. It seemed like even my physical workspace was fighting against me, resisting a new campus minister, conspiring to make me weary before I had begun. In addition to this, I thought the poop all over my office was symbolically showing me what I was about to make of this ministry, so my insecurities were exacerbated by my own negative thoughts. I wondered if my attempt to be a minister was all a sham covered in sewage.

I prayed that night for clarity. I prayed for courage and for God to strengthen my resolve to do the work before me. As I sat up that night, confused and worried, I believe God helped me to focus my mind. I kept seeing the image of a woman named Wanda who had helped me clean up the mess in my office. Wanda helped the campus minister before me, and the one before him. She had been the backbone and the rock of the student center for many years. It occurred to me while I was praying that I was not in this battle alone.

I would attribute this one incident to the foundational cornerstone that began my ministry. It is simply this: God has designed us to be in relationship with one another. Setbacks and mishaps will happen. Insecurities and self-doubt are part of human nature. People will resist change and try to wear you down. My recommendation is to surround yourself with positive people. Avoid listening to negative people. Make time for healing and soul recuperation. And above all, pray earnestly, deeply, and steadfastly. Those were some tough months, but when I slowed down and began to flesh out the plan that you have now read about in this book, the real signs of what could be began to take shape.

As I come to the final pages of this book, I want to share one more personal story with you. The reason I'm sharing this is to demonstrate how our personal testimonies can show the power of Christ working in our lives. Like I said, it was my second day on the job. I was covered in poop, wondering if I had made the right decision. As the months passed, I continued to have doubts, but I threw myself into the work anyway, and despite my inexperience, the ministry was beginning to grow. Students were giving their lives to Christ. Wanda was there working beside me, helping students navigate the tumultuous times of college life. Our ministry was finally coming together. If one thing is for certain, it is Satan always attacks when things are going well, and that is exactly what happened. I can only explain the next phase as a supernatural battle. The student center was winning souls, and this must have enraged Satan.

I was about two years into this new job when the city fire marshal showed up on our doorstep. After a long inspection, he deemed our house hazardous due to a variety of issues. The biggest problem was that we did not have any fire suppression. In short, we needed to retrofit a sprinkler system in our building, or the city was going to make us close the doors. A few weeks after this, a structural engineer for the city arrived. He also inspected our facility and determined it was not structurally sound and major modifications were needed to allow people inside. The good news is that we were given a reasonable timeline to complete these needed repairs. The bad news is that the repairs exceeded $250,000. We did what we could to raise the money, but in the end, we had only scratched the surface of what was needed.

I wish I could tell you that I was hopeful and optimistic, but that is not the truth. Just when things had seemed to be headed in the right direction, we got sucker punched. I felt defeated. All my doubts and insecurities from that second day on the job came crashing down on me. The words of one of the church leaders who was part of the team that hired me kept coming to mind. In essence, he had questioned (lovingly and with genuine concern) why I had left a stable, good-paying job to take on this work. No company incentives, insurance, or other perks. I was wondering the same thing.

The leadership of our church called a meeting, and I gave them the bad news. My financial projections provided no way to raise the rest of the money in the time we had left. The CSC was going to close for the first time in its history, and I was at the helm, only a couple of years into the work. I had no other job prospects on the horizon. I felt like a failure. The elders asked me what my plan was, and I will never forget the sinking feeling I had in my gut as we all sat around the table in silence.

The only answer I had was one word. I looked up at them and said, "Pray."

15

ARE WE THERE YET?

I f you like sports analogies, there is none better or more accurate than this one: the CSC was in the bottom of the ninth inning with two outs. It was almost game over. We had less than six months not only to come up with a quarter of a million dollars, but also to make the needed repairs before students arrived at school for fall semester.

I wish I could remember exactly how long after the meeting it was when one of our church leaders called me on the phone. It wasn't very long, though, maybe less than a month. I had been praying almost nonstop for a miracle. The conversation is fuzzy now, but it went something like this.

"Hey, Craig, I have some really good news."

Okay, so right here I want to stop and tell you about God working in powerful ways despite our lack of faith. In my situation, this was a case where God did not call the qualified, but rather, he qualified the called. Because what I should have thought at that moment was that God had answered my bold prayers of finding a way for our ministry to stay open. Instead, I thought the good news was something completely unrelated to the CSC. It wasn't a stretch of the imagination to think I was about to be out of a job, so maybe this was about another job opportunity.

"Really?" I said. "What is it?"

"Well, we just got a letter stating that a person who passed away left us some money in their will."

I was silent. I'm pretty sure I was holding my breath.

"Craig, are you still there?"

"Yeah, I'm here. So does that mean anything for the CSC?"

I heard him laugh a little. "Yes, it does. This person has donated a third of their estate, and his will stipulated that the money being given to us must be used specifically for the CSC."

So let me stop again and tell you, to my shame, that I was still thinking small. I thought that maybe we were talking about $25,000 to $50,000 at the most. Not nearly enough to do the needed repairs, but who knew? Maybe we could get someone to match the donation since we might have a good start. That still did not resolve the time issue we were facing. I was not hopeful that the needed repairs could be done before students returned.

I asked, "So are you allowed to tell me how much we have to work with?"

He paused a moment before saying, "I don't have the exact amount, but I know that it is more than $500,000."

I was stunned. Speechless. My eyes filled with tears. "Lord, please forgive my doubt!"

I heard his voice, but my ears were ringing. "Sorry, what did you say?"

"What do you want to do with the money?"

There was no pause in my reply. "I want to rebuild the entire student center for the next generation!"

There is more to the story. How just the right contractor showed up at the exact moment and was the only one who said he could demolish and rebuild our student center in less than four months. Every other contractor said it would take at least eighteen months to complete. Even in this, we had Satan hurling everything he could to knock us off course. We ran into remediation issues. We had more structural issues than we first thought. A worker was seriously injured when a brick column collapsed on him. Work had to be stopped due to the main sewer line under our building being compromised. It had to be replaced, and the street had to be busted up. Our entire front support wall collapsed. Even with all this, we were only two weeks late in opening our facility to students.

Since that day, amazing things have continued to happen. I wish I could say that every year has been smooth sailing, but the fact is that most years have been rough sailing. However, I have come to learn that this is a very strong indicator that we are bringing massive hurt and causing major damage to the legions that Satan is bringing against us. Not to get too dramatic, but I firmly believe that if we could, for just a moment, pull back the shroud that separates this physical life from the spiritual, and look down upon our building on the west side of the university campus, one would see a massive war being fought between angels and demons, and our student center is ground zero. Too much has happened for me to pass it all off as coincidence. We are bringing the fight to Satan, and I know he is enraged at our success.

I have full assurance that the CSC stands as a massive beacon of light in the darkness of our campus. Because of this, I am also aware that Satan is throwing whatever he can to extinguish that light. As a matter of fact, I am writing this paragraph at home on December 2, 2021, and it is 7:01 p.m. Thursday evening. I am battle weary because it has been a horrible week, and I am dealing with several spiritual wounds to some of our students. I am dazed and a bit shell-shocked, but even in this moment, I have learned God will always provide, and putting my faith in Him is never misplaced. We may not understand God's timing, but it is always right. We may not understand the bigger picture, but I know God's plan is also perfect, so I will trust in Him and have complete assurance that He has it all figured out.

I do not mind sharing this reality of our journey. The truth is this battle can be tough, exhausting, and even depressing at times. We need to understand that Jesus was absolutely *not* joking when He said that we need to count the cost and carry our cross. Listen to the words of James: "Count it all joy, my brothers, when you meet trials of various kinds, for you know that the testing of your faith produces steadfastness. And let steadfastness have its full effect, that you may be perfect and complete, lacking in nothing." (James 1:2–4)

This road that we are on as believers is becoming less traveled. Being a Christian is not for the weak. It requires dedication and resolve despite the failures. We fall, we get back up. We fall again, we get back up again. We keep moving forward. We keep marching on. We pick up the wounded along the way. But what we don't do is go into the battle lacking the knowledge and the protection that God is giving to us. In part, that is really what this whole book has been about: giving you some glimpses into what the battle looks like from your child's perspective. Letting you know what they are up against—what you are up against—and how best to fight this battle. We are not there yet. This is a lifelong journey where every mile we gain is a mile that was gained by pushing hard, despite the fatigue and injuries.

As I close out, know that I am praying for all of you who are willing to learn and understand the enemy, to implement the battle strategy and recruitment techniques that Jesus taught us, to remain steadfast against the deniers who will revolt against these proven strategies, and to walk headlong into the battle and fight for our youth and for every brother and sister that stands beside us. Will it not be an awesome thing, that when we reach the end of this journey, we can say:

I have fought the good fight, I have finished the race, I have kept the faith. Henceforth there is laid up for me the crown of righteousness, which the Lord, the righteous judge, will award to me on that Day, and not only to me but also to all who have loved his appearing. (2 Timothy 4:7–8)

APPENDIX 1

Questions for Small Groups

The following pages were sent to me by Don Nickens who served with Manna Global Ministries in the Dominican Republic some years ago. I had the pleasure of meeting Don when I took a college group there for a mission trip. I immediately became deeply intrigued by the discipling methods that MGM were using because they were practicing a very similar method to what we had been using at the CSC. I have used these questions not only in discipling groups but have also taught several discipling classes using this exact handout.

Key passages: Proverbs 25:12; 27:17; Ecclesiastes 4:8–12; Romans 14:13–23; 2 Corinthians 12:19–13:6; Galatians 6:1–6; Colossians 3:16; Ephesians 4:9–13; 1 Thessalonians 5:14; James 5:15–16; Hebrews 3:13

> Therefore confess your sins to each other and pray for each other so that you may be healed. The prayer of a righteous man is powerful and effective. (James 5:15–16)

Accountability allows us to be answerable to one another, with the focus on improving our key relationships with people such as our spouse, close friends, colleagues, coworkers, a boss, small group members, or a pastor. Accountability will also enhance our integrity, maturity, character relationships in general, and our growth in Christ. Accountability is sharing, in confidence, our heartfelt Christian sojourn in an atmosphere of trust so we can give an answer for what we do, see where we need help, understand our struggles where we are weak, and be encouraged to stay on track, seek prayer, care, and support when we fail as well as model guideposts for one another to keep us going.

Below are some key accountability questions you can ask yourself or have a mentor ask you. These are designed for small groups and mentoring for those from high school youth to seasoned adults. They are for men's groups, women's groups, and so forth. Because of the number of questions, all you need to do is choose three or four questions for each week. If there is a particular area of struggle, add that one, too. Also, incorporate one of the key passages above and spend significant time in prayer:

1. Did you spend significant time with God through His Word, prayer, quiet time, devotions, and other spiritual disciplines? How much? How constant? Is He your driving force?
2. What blocks your growth in Christ? What blocks growth, in your other relationships, from becoming more mature and effectual?
3. How has your time with God been? Did you pray for others? Are you satisfied with the time you spent with our Lord this week? How so? What can you do to improve it? Did you pray for the others in this group?
4. Have you faithfully served the Lord, His people, and the lost?
5. Did you participate in church activities and worship this week? How so? Why not?
6. Did you set spiritual goals this week? What were they? Did you achieve your spiritual goals?
7. Have you made your family a priority? What noteworthy activity or deed did you do for your spouse or family?
8. How have you struggled with sin? What are the sins that have weighed down your walk with God this week?
9. What did you do to enhance your relationship with your spouse/friends? What can you do to make that relationship better?

10. In what ways has God blessed you this week? How have you shared your blessings?

11. What disappointments did you face? Did they consume your thoughts? What did you do about it? What can you learn?

12. Have you filled the mandates of your call, work, and school, practicing excellence, and being the best 100 percent as you can be for His glory?

13. Have you committed any sexual sin? Did you look at someone lustfully? Have you been alone in a compromising situation? Have you been flirtatious? Have you struggled with pornography or "romance novels?" Have you exposed yourself to any sexually oriented material? Did you put yourself in a situation with a member of the opposite sex that could appear to be compromising, even though it may not have been?

14. Have you shared your faith? In what ways? How can you improve? Have you had an opportunity to share with a non-Christian?

15. How well are you handling your finances right now? Have your financial dealings been questionable?

16. Have you been trustworthy? Have you lied? Stolen? Cheated? Been dishonest or manipulative? Have you elevated yourself over another for your own personal agenda? What about your language and attitude?

17. Have you allowed the media and its distortions in TV, music, and movies to unduly influence you? What about peer pressure?

18. Have you been prideful? Have you been guilty of gossip or anger? Slandered? Shown indifference? Been greedy? Not controlled your tongue? This hinders people from knowing and trusting Christ the most!

19. Have you demonstrated a servant's heart? How so? What have you done for someone else this week?

20. Did you struggle with a disappointment this week? How did you handle it?

21. Have you respected and treated your classmates, coworkers, and peers graciously by showing them compassion and the love of God in your words and deeds? What can you do to enhance your relationships here?
22. How is your level of character, according to the comparison of Galatians 5:22–23 vs. Galatians 5:19–21?
23. How did you practice joy this week? Have you had a thankful attitude toward God? Have you struggled with anger toward God? How so? What can you do about it?
24. Have you taken care of the temple of the Holy Spirit with rest, sleep, exercise, healthy eating, etc.? What about addictions, gluttony, or substance abuse?
25. Have your thoughts been kept pure?
26. Are you giving to the Lord's work with your time, talent, and treasures? What about financially?
27. What do you need to do to improve your relationships with God and with others?
28. What do you see as your number one need or struggle for this next week?
29. Have you compromised your integrity in any way or lied about the above questions?
30. How can this group help you?

Take it slow and easy. Don't try, or even expect, to immediately delve into the deepest, darkest corners of your life. Begin by having your close friends hold you accountable for things like praying regularly and integrity issues. As you see the benefit and results of this, you will also be building up trust, which is necessary for accountability in more personal and private areas.

If you fall away from these questions, or refuse to have someone hold you to them, then Satan will have a foothold in your life. These questions are not just for the pastor or church leader; they are for all Christians who want to live a life of integrity and significance. The failure to have accountability will produce sin. At that point, it is not a question of if you may fall, but, rather, when you will engage in sin and destroy everything in your life. The relationships and ministry God has given you as well as your family and those around you, for generations to come, will be destroyed. Yes, there can be restitution and restoration, but the cost can never be completely repaid. Just look at King David; his sin had dire consequences with which we still live.

The Christian life offers glaring, empirical proof that "all of us make many mistakes" (James 3:2), and we are grateful for the forgiveness offered to us through Jesus Christ (1 John 2:1).

APPENDIX 2

Tool Bag

ADDICTIONS AND COUNSELING RESOURCES

Alcohol
- Alcoholrehabguide.org: helpful links and information
- Alcohol.org: links to treatments and information
- *Codependent No More* by Melody Beattie

Drugs
- Therecoveryvillage.com: resources and information

Eating Disorders
- Nationaleatingdisorders.org
- Eatingrecoverycenter.com
- Eatingdisorderhope.com
- Anad.org

Pornography
- Foryourmarriage.org: a site with many other resources
- Oceanrecoverycentre.com: lots of helpful links and information
- *Fight for Love* by Rosie Makinney: an insightful book about porn addiction

Counseling
- Counseling.org: American Counseling Association with links to mental health resources

DISCIPLING RESOURCES

Books
- *The Cost of Discipleship* by Dietrich Bonhoeffer
- *Kingdom Disciples* by Tony Evans
- *The Impossible Mentor* by Ray Hollenbach

Links
- StudentsofJesus.com

INSIGHTFUL BOOKS FOR PARENTS, MINISTERS, AND CHURCH LEADERS

- *Mere Christianity* by C.S. Lewis
- *Sticky Faith* by Chap Clark and Kara Powell
- *Radical: Taking Back Your Faith from the American Dream* by David Platt
- *Your Child's Journey* by Jay Austin
- *Generation iY* by Tim Elmore
- *The Benedict Option* by Rod Dreher
- *Surprising Insights from the Unchurched* by Thom Rainer
- *The Case for Christ* by Lee Strobel

QUESTIONS TO ASK THE CAMPUS MINISTER AT YOUR CHILD'S UNIVERSITY

1. Do you have a specific program or model that you use to share the gospel/strengthen your students' faith?
2. Do you have student leaders and if so, what do they do?
3. What is the average size of your events?
4. What kind of support does your ministry have from the university?
5. How are you funded?
6. What does your ministry do on weekly basis?
7. Do you teach any Bible classes?

8. How often do you or your students have one-on-one Bible studies?
9. What percentage of your graduates have remained faithful?
10. What do you see as your ministries' biggest concerns?
11. What outreach ministries do you provide for students?
12. Do you have retreats?
13. Does your ministry provide opportunities for local mission work?
14. What about short-term mission trips abroad?
15. Does your ministry have small groups?
16. How are the small groups structured/organized/led?
17. How often does your ministry eat together?
18. Can you tell me about any monthly events or activities you have?
19. What is your main objective?
20. Why did you become a campus minister?

Obviously these are just some suggested questions that parents might want to know about a campus ministry at your child's university. There are many other questions that you can ask, and this list is merely a baseline of ones that have stood out to me over the years. Some of these questions are also good to ask the local church where your child may be attending while in college. I would encourage you to visit the church and campus ministry as often as possible.

NOTES

1. Jeffrey M. Jones, "U.S. Church Membership Falls Below Majority for First Time," March 29, 2021, news.gallup.com/poll/341963/church-membership-falls-below-majority-first-time.aspx.

2. Rod Dreher, *The Benedict Option: A Strategy for Christians in a Post-Christian Nation* (New York, Sentinel, 2017), 112.

3. Brian Crosby, "Giving up Gimmicks: Reclaiming Youth Ministry from an Entertainment Culture," The Gospel Coalition, 2012, thegospelcoalition.org/themelios/review/giving-up-gimmicks-reclaiming-youth-ministry-from-an-entertainment-culture/.

4. Dave Ramsey, "Outrageous Generosity is the most fun you will ever have with money," Twitter, December 12, 2016, 7:32 a.m., twitter.com/DaveRamsey/status/808288430652264448.

5. Dave Ramsey, "You'll never be happy if you chase money and stuff all of your life, but you can find true joy through giving and serving others," Twitter, October 3, 2014, 8:22 a.m., twitter.com/HumaniTV/status/518028208319758336/photo/1.

6. Dave Ramsey, "Money is a wonderful tool, but it makes a terrible god. Build wealth to use and help others, not to worship," Twitter, June 12, 2022, 12:12 p.m., twitter.com/DaveRamsey/status/1536018489118445569.

7. Megan Neff and Mark McMinn, *Embodying Integration* (Downers Grove, IL: InterVarsity Press, 2020), 132.

8. Diana Baumrind, "Effects of Authoritative Parental Control on Child Behavior," *Child Development* 37, no. 4 (December 1966): 887–907.

9. Sam Louie, "Minority Report Pastors and Porn: Why Many Pastors Suffer in Silence and Secrecy," Psychology Today, January 30, 2020, psychologytoday.com/us/blog/minority-report/202001/pastors-and-porn.

10. Ibid.

11. Adam Alter, *Irresistible: The Rise of Addictive Technology and the Business of Keeping Us Hooked* (New York: Penguin Press, 2017), 2.

12. C. S. Lewis, *Surprised by Joy: The Shape of My Early Life* (London: Geoffrey Bles, 1955), 207–208.

13. intimacywithgod.wordpress.com/2008/09/11/this-theme-of-intimacy/.

14. Bobby Ross, Jr., "Revisiting the Boston Movement: ICOC Growing Again After Crisis," *The Christian Chronicle*, September 1, 2012, christianchronicle.org/revisiting-the-boston-movement-icoc-growing-again-after-crisis/.

15. forbes.com/sites/johnbbrandon/2020/03/04/67-million-people-just-mentioned-the-coronavirus-on-social-media-in-one-day-heres-why/?sh=7f4bc1d25eb1.

16. Phyllis Tickle, *The Great Emergence: How Christianity Is Changing and Why* (Grand Rapids, MI: Baker Books, 2008), 16.

17. P. C. Wagner, *Church Quake! How the New Apostolic Reformation Is Shaking the Church as We Know It* (Glendale, CA: Regal Books, 1982), 36.

18. Jerry Pillay, "COVID-19 Shows the Need to Make Church More Flexible," *Sage Journals* 37, no. 4 (2020): 271, doi.org/10.1177/0265378820963156.

19. Wolfgang Simpson, *Houses That Change the World: The Return of the House Churches* (UK: OM Publishing, 1999), 34.

20. C. J. P. Niemandt (lecture, International Fresh Expressions of Church Conference, Cape Town, South Africa, February 2016).

ABOUT THE AUTHOR

CRAIG ALLISON currently lives in Northwest Georgia with his wife and three semi-grown children in an old house that they are constantly restoring. Craig currently works as a campus minister for the University of Tennessee at Chattanooga where he spends his time ministering to college students. He hosts a podcast called, *The Lion, the Way, and the War* where he discusses Jesus, His church, and the spiritual battle that surrounds us all. He frequently interviews college students, new Christians, authors, church leaders, and even the occasional politician. The podcast can be heard on all major podcast services. Send questions and comments to thelionthewaythewar@gmail.com.

Made in United States
Orlando, FL
08 May 2023

32928524R00104